T0199250

Understanding Blockchain and Cryptocurrencies

Understanding Blockchain and Cryptocurrencies

A Primer for Implementing and Developing Blockchain Projects

Akira Summers

CRC Press
Taylor & Francis Group
Boca Raton London New York

CRC Press is an imprint of the
Taylor & Francis Group, an **Informa** business

First edition published 2022
by CRC Press
6000 Broken Sound Parkway NW, Suite 300, Boca Raton, FL 33487-2742

and by CRC Press
2 Park Square, Milton Park, Abingdon, Oxon, OX14 4RN

© 2022 Taylor & Francis Group, LLC

CRC Press is an imprint of Taylor & Francis Group, LLC

ISBN: 9781032034065 (hbk)
ISBN: 9781032034072 (pbk)
ISBN: 9781003187165 (ebk)

DOI: 10.1201/9781003187165

Typeset in Sabon
by Newgen Publishing UK

This book is dedicated to my darling children, Dantai, Skyler and Rayven; to Rei; to my partner, James Gordon; to my sisters Donna Dixon and Shelley McCubbin; to the friends who have supported me over the years, in no particular order, Melissa Reddy, Damian Rourke, Helena Nouwens, Stacy O'Brien, John Kelly, Avi Jawanda, Lianne Forbes, Valentina Ippolito, Cathy Easthope, Sander Sarti, Ben Clempson and to my Granny and Peter.

Contents

Figures

About the author

Hi, I am Akira Summers and I have been working in software and techno-
logical development since the year 2000. I started off in web development
and interactive media, but I have held many development roles including
spending several years working as a game programmer.

I am a lecturer in digital media technologies at Birmingham City University
in the United Kingdom, teaching programming, interactive media and
development. I am a keen blockchain developer and researcher, teaching
students and industrial partners the joy of blockchain and supporting them
in their blockchain endeavours. When I began developing for blockchain
and teaching my students, I struggled to find books that brought together
the different things that they needed to understand, so I decided to write my
own and I hope you enjoy it!

Preface

So, you want to learn about blockchain. Good move! Blockchains are still in their early days and activity is growing year by year. We are in a comparable stage to the internet in its infancy. It was seen as transformational, but it was just getting going. In the beginning, static webpages were all you could expect. Now, we have interactive web applications and all manner of different technologies built on top of the internet, from apps on mobile phones, to smart devices connected around the home.

Right now, there are hundreds, probably thousands of blockchain networks, but the potential is still growing day by day and new use-cases emerge that not only revise and enhance existing tools and workflows but also allow for innovations from blockchain-based, censorship-resistant social media, to game asset management.

With so much happening and so many opportunities emerging, right now is a very exciting time to be learning about blockchain and getting involved in developing or managing projects that use this innovative new technology.

This is a guide to the basic principles of how blockchains work. There are many different implementations of blockchains and this number is growing rapidly. The cryptocurrency field alone has thousands of unique blockchains, each with their own purpose and features that are often devised and created by thriving communities of developers. It is impossible to write one guide that covers all of the features of all existing blockchains. This book, instead, covers the general principles that apply, though they are modified in different implementations.

In this book, you will learn about the structure of a blockchain and the principles that it is built upon. You will look at the methods employed in cryptocurrencies and the structures and techniques used in managing transactions. We will look at so-called blockchain 1.0 and blockchain 2.0, the differences and vulnerabilities. We will discuss and explain topics such as hashing, Merkle trees, nodes, mining, Proof of Work and Proof of Stake, consensus mechanisms, encryption and much more.

Who is this book for?

Though this book describes the computing concepts behind the blockchain, it is not *just* for developers. Of course, if you want to move into blockchain management of supply chains or are responsible for a blockchain voting system, you really should understand what is happening inside these systems. Equally, if you would like to manage blockchain projects, then you should have a grounding in the concepts and possibilities that blockchains bring.

This book is intended to act as a primer, before possibly moving onto further study in follow-on subjects such as blockchain development, blockchain for business, financial technologies/FinTech, supply chain management or any of the many and varied roles that are growing around this new technology.

Acknowledgement

I would like to thank those who have contributed to the making of this book. In particular, I would like to thank Manyee Lee, John Lee and Damian Rourke, for the insightful feedback that I received from you. Additionally, I would like to thank Dr Gavin Wood, founder of Ethereum and Parity, Rob Stupay and The Remix Project, TradingView and BitInfoCharts for allowing me to use your images, charts and data.

Notes

Notes and interesting facts are provided in the following boxes. It is not essential to read them to understand blockchains, but they provide useful context and fun facts like this:

> Note: Satoshi Nakamoto, the inventor of the first real-world, widely used blockchain, never actually used the term blockchain. It was coined years later. He instead referred to it as a chain-of-blocks.

The wonderful world of blockchain is shrouded in mystery, its inventor being anonymous, releasing the idea and the source code through a pseudonym. It is easy to see why the inventor of a disruptive technology might want to remain anonymous, particularly when the system you are disrupting is money!

Here is another fun fact:

> Note: No man is an island, and Nakamoto's Bitcoin paper builds on the work already done by Bell Lab's Stuart Haber and Scott Stornetta in their work, "How to time-stamp a digital document," in *Journal of Cryptology*, vol 3, no 2, pages 99–111, 1991. This was referenced in Satoshi Nakamoto's white paper, "Bitcoin: A Peer-to-Peer Electronic Cash System", available at https://Bitcoin.org/Bitcoin.pdf

Right, it is time to get on with the business of learning all about how blockchains work.

What should you know before reading this book?

Not much! You don't need to know how to program – there is no programming in this book at all. We look at the key concepts from the beginning and work our way up. As blockchains are fundamentally a computing-based technology, a general understanding of computing will be very useful.

You will find that different implementations of blockchains use different terminology for the same things. This is unavoidable, but to help, I have provided a list below with key terms and definitions that you should be comfortable with before reading.

KEY TERMS TO KNOW BEFORE READING

Immutability

Being immutable and therefore impossible to change or destroy.

Hexadecimal

Also known as base-16, or hex. It is a method of representing numbers using a base of 16. Whereas decimal represents numbers with 10 digits, hexadecimal uses 16, using numbers 0–9 and then continuing to A–F, so that A=10, B=11, C=12, D=13, E=14, F=15 and 10=16.

Protocol

A collection of rules and conventions that define data structures, formatting methods and other aspects of a particular system.

Metadata

Data that describes other data. A digital image, for example, is a collection of colour information, relating to each pixel. Metadata is often stored in image files that describe that data and could include the photographer, the camera used and the aperture.

Fiat currency

Money that has no intrinsic value. Unlike gold coins, whose value is derived from the substance that they are made of, Fiat money's value is derived from the government that issues it and mutual agreement on its value by those who use it.

Ledger

A document of transactions including credits and debits and balances of accounts.

Server

A computer system or program that provides data or services to other computers or programs. A web server, for example, hosts the content and when a browser is used to connect to the server, the server provides that content to the browser for display.

Client

A computer system or program that accesses data or services made available by a server. A web client, for example, would connect to a web server and download the content of the web pages, then display it to the user.

Client-side/server-side

In server and client systems, we will often refer to activities taking place on the client as being client-side and activities taking place on the server being server-side. This can be an important distinction – for example, when working with secure information, we would need to be considerate about where in the client-server model that information is processed.

Front-end/back-end

The front-end of an application refers to the interface or presentation layer. The back-end of an application refers to the data-processing parts of the application. In the client-server model, generally, front-end aspects are done on the client-side and back-end aspects take place on the server-side. This is a generalization, rather than a rule.

Binary

Binary is a numbering system of base-2, where there are only two states for each digit, 0 or 1. Any number can be represented using the system, where:

000	0	010	2	100	4	110	6
001	1	011	3	101	5	111	7

Figure 0.1 Binary code example.

Why learn about blockchains?

Blockchains are a disruptive technology comparable to the internet. When the internet arrived, it changed almost every aspect of everyday life. Blockchains are doing that in a range of areas, from finance to games. When a new technology comes along that changes everything, those who understand the technology are at a great advantage.

The blockchain sector is booming. Every day you hear of new applications of the blockchain and new implementations. The announcement of new cryptocurrencies and unique features seems to grow daily in pace, and it seems every country in the world is showing signs of developing digital versions of their currency, from the digital dollar to the digital yuan.

Since blockchain's inception as a tool for finance, many other applications have emerged. It has great potential for use in supply chains, currency and asset management, voting and Digital Rights Management – to establish ownership and provenance.

The number of job opportunities working on blockchains is growing fast. Blockchain-related understanding and ability are some of the most exciting and in-demand skills – and if you want to work with blockchains, then having a good understanding of what they are and how they work is essential.

Chapter 1

What are blockchains for?

PROVENANCE AND TRUST

A key feature of blockchains is that they allow you to manage and verify the history of an asset, removing the necessity to trust in a supplier. In doing this, they allow you to establish ownership or proof of origin.

One way in which they stand out from other data types, such as conventional databases, is that they are immutable. That is to say that once something has been added to a well-functioning blockchain it is practically impossible to change it. We will talk later about how a blockchain achieves this immutability.

Let's look at an example of a supply chain managed by a blockchain and how this works to eliminate the need to trust. As they say in the blockchain community, *don't trust, verify*.

Let's assume I am manufacturing cars. I claim that my car has been made using only high-quality, safety-tested and compliant components (fig 1.1).

Normally as a manufacturer, I have to trust those people who provide me with parts to supply the parts that I have ordered, to the specifications that I have required and anyone who receives a car from me has to trust me in the same way. The truth is that they could quite easily switch to using cheaper, less regulated sources for their components and I might not be able to tell (fig 1.2). I must trust them.

Instead, consider an alternative where the whole supply chain is managed through a blockchain (fig 1.3). Because blockchains offer a way in which we can track the components and their history and this data cannot be changed and is available to see throughout the process, we no longer need to trust in the supplier, we can verify using the blockchain.

In this situation, all the individual manufacturers can check where each of their products has come from, the resources that they were made with, as well as when they were delivered and other information related to the supply. It would not be possible for a manufacturer to claim that their product was made from something that it was not, at it would be easily visible to everyone when they consulted the blockchain.

DOI: 10.1201/9781003187165-1

1

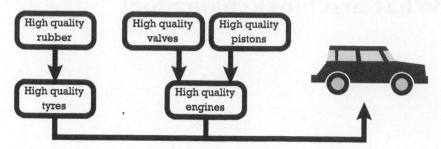

Figure 1.1 Product supply chain.

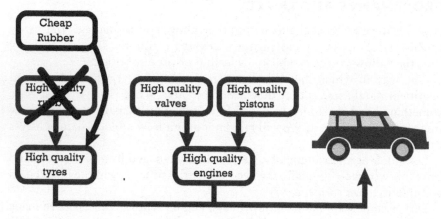

Figure 1.2 Dishonest supply chain.

DOWNTIME

Blockchains are available 24 hours a day, 7 days a week and 365 days a year. Because they don't require people to operate the system in the same way that comparable systems do, they can provide a continuous service.

Because of the level of validation checking, and the decentralized approach, they are very robust and resistant to attack. In an age of hacking, identity theft and cyber-attacks increased security is a greatly desirable trait.

They can drastically reduce the amount of administrative overhead and in doing so create great cost savings. Their increased transparency makes auditing easier and fraud more difficult. All these benefits and more are derived from the blockchain's unique approach to data storage and transmission. This approach, the structures, methods and rules that it comprises are all part of the blockchain protocol. We will start by looking at the data structures employed and move onto the networking and transmission.

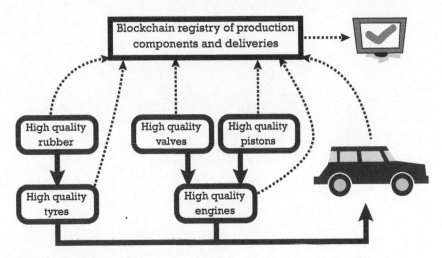

Figure 1.3 Blockchain supply chain.

NOT FOR EVERYTHING

Blockchains can be very powerful. They are however not for everything. There are certainly some downsides to using blockchains. They can be resource hungry for example, when compared to other methods of storing and working with data. One of the first questions that you should be asking as a developer or project manager is whether a blockchain is needed for your system. As you read through this book and learn more about blockchains, you will develop an understanding of the strengths of blockchains and the associated costs, so that you can answer that question.

Key points about blockchain uses

- Blockchains allow for trustless relationships.
- They can be used to establish provenance.
- They have many applications.
- They are resilient against issues with downtime.

Chapter 2

Basic principles of blockchain

BLOCK STRUCTURE

There are many features of a blockchain. To make things easy to understand, we will start with a highly simplified model and gradually add and explain additional features, to build up our conceptual model.

At its simplest, blockchains store information by chunking data into blocks and linking them. This is not a new concept in computing. At this level, a linked list (fig 2.1) works in a similar manner, though there are many important differences which we will discuss.

With linked lists, each node contains data and a pointer to the location of the next node. Blockchains work in a slightly different way. The following diagram shows the contents of a Bitcoin block (fig 2.2).

With blockchains, each block contains an amount of data and is linked to the previous block. Often blocks are compared to the pages of a book, the complete book being the blockchain and the data sitting inside the page.

Each block in addition to the data contained also includes a header consisting of several pieces of *metadata* about the block. We will explore the structure of this header as we build up our understanding of the blocks and the blockchain that they form.

The blocks are stored as files. They are indexed by a separate index file, outside of the chain, together with other useful information for the system. Bitcoin, for example, has a blkindex.dat file which contains an index of the block files. Block data are stored in the blk000n.dat file, where 000n is the number of the block (fig 2.3).

Though they are present in blockchains, we will generally leave this indexing information off from future diagrams, to keep them simple.

By separating the link to the next block and instead indexing the information in a separate file, this means that the data of the previous block does not need to change, in order to add a point to the next block. Maintaining data, without change, is a key feature of blockchains.

We know that for blockchains to be useful, the data stored inside it needs to be fixed and immutable. Linked lists by themselves do not, however,

DOI: 10.1201/9781003187165-2

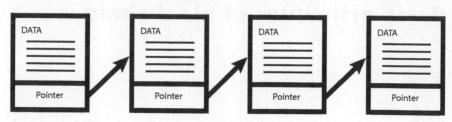

Figure 2.1 Linked lists.

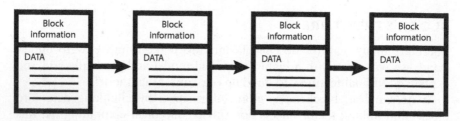

Figure 2.2 Beginning blockchain.

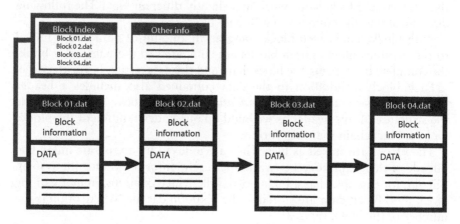

Figure 2.3 Blockchain with index.

ensure that data cannot change. In this situation, it would be possible to open up the data inside the block and modify it so it would not be immediately obvious that this had happened. In order to be able to verify its contents and ensure the integrity of the data contained we need to use hashing. Hashing is central to the functionality of a blockchain so let's investigate it.

Key points about blocks

- Blockchains are a linked chain of information chunked into blocks.
- Once something is written into the blockchain it should not be changed.
- Each block contains data and metadata about the block.

HASHING

Hashing is the name given to a process whereby you input data and from that receive a value in return. The output you receive back is of a fixed length and always the same length, regardless of the amount of data you input (fig 2.4).

The hashing is done by a computer algorithm. Generally, we can consider them as a black box. That is to say, we don't need to worry too much on a day-to-day basis, how exactly this is being achieved, we just need to understand the principles of what is taking place.

The output from a hash function is a very long number, but it is usually represented as an alphanumeric value, to make it easier to read, transmit and work with.

```
4FAD1A2214C4A7B1F0325A9F8B8541DF = 1059078090663695
                                   411422107393654
                                   34704351
```

Figure 2.4 Hash function.

HASH REPRESENTED AS HEXADECIMAL AND DECIMAL NUMBERS

If we run the same data into the same algorithm, we will always get the same output. If, however, that data changes even slightly, the resulting hash will be completely different. Even a small change, like a capitalization, will result in a different hash (fig 2.5).

For this reason, a hash is often referred to as a fingerprint of the data. We can use the hash value to check that the data hasn't changed at all. In this example, we will use the obligatory naming convention of Alice and Bob, at least for now, and Bob sends Alice a message. She wants to check to make sure the message was accurately sent (fig 2.6).

Bob creates the message, hashes that message and sends Alice both the message and the hash. Alice would be able to receive the message, hash it and check the two hashes against each other to make sure that the message had not been changed, by corruption or through somebody interfering with the message before it reached her.

Note: This does not offer much security against malicious changes because it would be relatively easy to rehash the message again afterwards. We discuss encryption later though.

There are many different types of hashing algorithm. They each produce different length hashes. The output hash is measured in the number of bits that the final value takes to store.

- MD5: Produces a 128-bit hash which can be used as a checksum. This is a value used to verify data integrity.

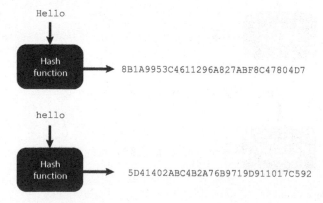

Figure 2.5 Small differences of input.

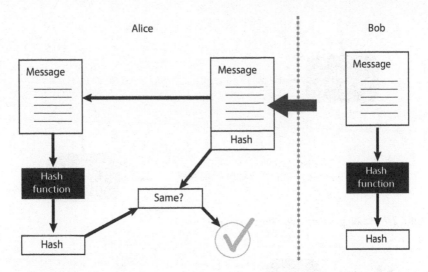

Figure 2.6 Hash for verification.

- SHA 2: A family of hash functions produced by the National Security Agency (NSA) with a variety of hash lengths. SHA-256 is one of these commonly used in blockchains.
- Keccak-256: provides a 256-bit hash and is and is currently used in some blockchains.

Note: Bitcoin uses a hashing algorithm called SHA-256

Note: The hashes in the examples above were made with the MD5 hashing algorithm. It was made for encrypting but security vulnerabilities have been found with it though, so it is only really used for less consequential error checking now.

Another important feature of hash functions is that it is relatively easy computationally, to go from the input to the output. It is, however, very difficult indeed, to the point of being practically impossible, to go from the output back to the input.

Note: Though it is technically possible to determine the possible input from the output, it requires greater computing power than we have, to solve this at this time. This may change when quantum computing power becomes available.

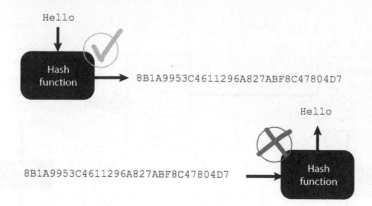

Figure 2.7 Hashing is a one-way function.

Figure 2.8 Unknown input for hash.

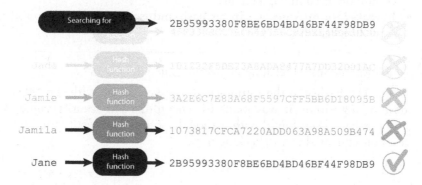

Figure 2.9 Brute force.

Let's look at an example. If, for example, I provide you with the hash of a first name, you know that it has been made using SHA-256 because that is what the system uses (fig 2.8).

If you wanted to determine what the value was, the most effective way of doing this would be to start hashing known names and checking to see if the hashes matched. This is known as *brute force* (fig 2.9).

Though it will probably take many guesses, eventually you will likely find out the name. Consider, now, that I have provided you with the hash of a list of 20 names. Finding out the input list becomes vastly more difficult. How about if I give you a list of 20 randomly generated words? The options now are so large that it would take many, many years to determine the answer by brute force. We can see therefore that so long as the data input is large and varied, we can consider the hash to be secure.

COLLISIONS

You may have considered that given the data can be vastly larger than the hash, then it must be possible to generate the same hash from two different sets of data. This is true. We call this a collision. The number of collisions depends on the length of the hash that we output. The smaller the hash output in length, the more likely a collision is. The longer the hash, the less likely.

The lengths of hashes that we use in blockchains mean that collisions are highly unlikely, so we can assume that if we are looking at the hash of a value A and we know that the hash of value B is the same, then A is the same as B (fig 2.10).

This in fact is typically how passwords are managed. Imagine you are running a website where users login. Because you don't want to store the passwords of all your users on your computers, in case someone gains access to the computer and steals the passwords, instead when your users set up their accounts, you store the hashes of the password (fig 2.11).

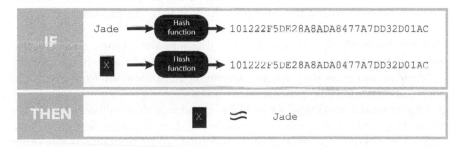

Figure 2.10 Matching hashes ≈ matching inputs.

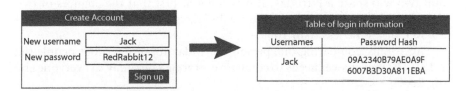

Figure 2.11 Password hash storage.

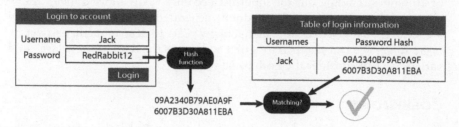

Figure 2.12 **Password hash check.**

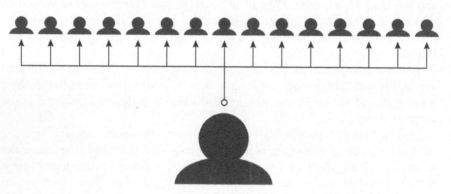

Figure 2.13 **One birthday comparison.**

When a user logs in, it checks the hash of the password the user entered against the hash stored for your password. If they are the same, the password entered is deemed to be correct (fig 2.12).

With this method, if someone gains access to the website database and retrieves the hash of users' passwords, they will not be able to gain access to their accounts as they cannot determine the password from the hash. Remember, the hashing process is one-way.

One potential weakness we need to consider is that collisions are likely to increase where the number of possible colliders increases. So far, we have looked at whether one individual hash is likely to be the same as any other given hash.

You may have heard that in a room of 30 people it is more likely than not that two will share a birthday. It may seem at first that the chances of two sharing a birthday given that there are 365 days in the year and 30 people is 30/365, or a little less than 10%.

This is only comparing one person's birthday to all the other people (fig 2.13). The real answer needs to compare everyone's birthday to everyone else (fig 2.14).

When adding in all these extra possible clashes we find it is actually nearer 70 per cent.

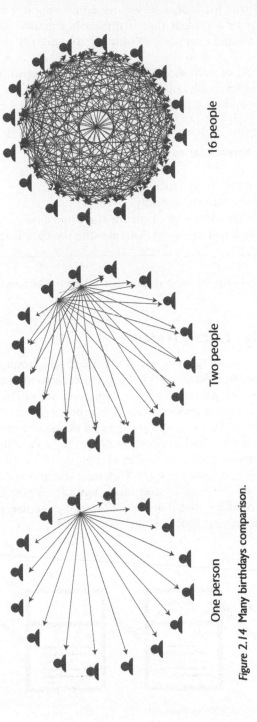

16 people

Two people

One person

Figure 2.14 Many birthdays comparison.

The same is true for hashes. If we are comparing one hash to one other hash, we could be confident that if the hashes match, the input matches. The more inputs and outputs we compare though, the more likely a clash is to occur.

The likelihood of a clash is very much dependent on the length of the hash, or, more specifically, number of possibilities for the hash. The longer the hash, the less likely a clash becomes.

Key points about hashes

- They are easy to produce
- They are effectively one-way
- They are the same every time for the same data
- Matching hashes mean we can assume the data is the same.

These features will become important when we discuss how they apply to blockchains.

HASHING IN BLOCKCHAINS

Blockchains use hashing in a few different places. Importantly, they use hashing to ensure that data is not changed after it is written to the blockchain. Let's look at the first and most simple implementation. Each block contains a hash of the data in the previous block, except for the first block, which has no previous block. This is called the genesis block and instead has a string of zeros. When a new block is added, it takes the hash of the previous block and writes it into itself. This is illustrated below.

This means that if someone were to change the information in block two for example, then the hash of that block would change. This would mean that the hash listed for that block would now be incorrect and that would invalidate the following block.

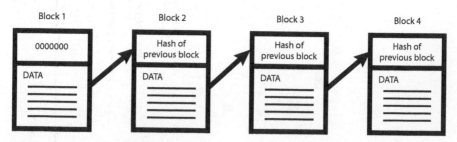

Figure 2.15 Blockchain with hashes.

If we were to go back even further and change something in block one, that would change its hash, which would invalidate the following block as its hash would now be changed, which would invalidate the following block to the current block. It becomes impossible to make a change to the content of any block without invalidating every block after it.

This alone does not stop tampering and creates the immutable data store that blockchain provides, but it is the first important step towards this. It would, at this stage in our blockchain journey, be possible to change the hashes in the entire chain. We will look at how this is addressed later, but for now, let's continue to explore the structure of the blockchain.

Blockchains commonly contain too much data to operate in the same way as linked lists. If each block contained just one piece of information the blockchain would grow to be unwieldy in a very short amount of time. Instead, the information inside each block is a chunk of data. Each item in this chunk is also hashed to prevent someone from going in and changing a single value. This is stored in the block as a Merkle root of the Merkle tree of the items. Let's look at what that means.

Key points hashing in blockchains

- Blockchains are chains of chunked data.
- The hash of the block is stored in the next block to help prevent later changes.
- Hashing is a one-way process that provides a digital fingerprint of the data.
- It is almost impossible to work out the original data from its hash.

MERKLE TREE

A Merkle tree is a structure built on hashing algorithms. As its name suggests, it is a tree-like structure where the leaves of the tree are hashes of pieces of data, normally drawn upside down from how one might expect a tree to appear (fig 2.16).

You can see that each of the leaves (at the bottom) are hashes of data. The hash of each two leaf pairs combined makes its parent node. They are then combined to make the next parent node until you end up at the root. If there is no pair to use then the same value is repeated, which generates a different hash again.

They afford us a method to verify the data that is contained in the tree. If any part of any of the data is changed, it will change the Merkle root.

In blockchains, the Merkle root is to allow the system to verify the contents of the block. The hashing of the contents of the block and the links between blocks helps to ensure that if anything changes at any point within any of the blocks, that block becomes invalid and is therefore rejected.

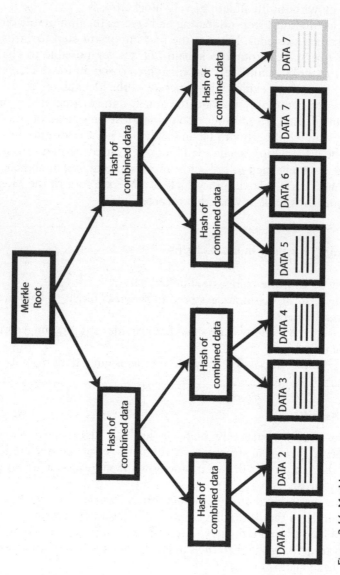

Figure 2.16 Merkle tree.

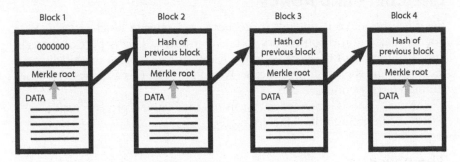

Figure 2.17 Blockchain with Merkle root.

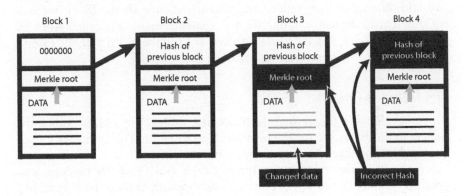

Figure 2.18 Blockchain with changes.

So now our blockchain looks like this (see fig 2.17).

So far, we have developed a chain of data, that if any part of the data is changed, it renders that block and the following blocks invalid (fig 2.18).

As we mentioned before though, on any one given system, a person might be able to change all of the information in the blockchain. There are a couple of mechanisms that help address this vulnerability. The first we will look at is difficulty.

Key points about Merkle trees

- Merkle trees are trees of hashes of the data contained in the block.
- They are useful for identifying changes that occur to the data in that block.
- Any change to a block after it is written in renders following blocks invalid.

DIFFICULTY AND NONCE

In order the make it difficult to go back and rewrite blocks, we make a system that requires some work to create a block. This is part of a mechanism called *Proof of Work*. Making it difficult to replace the blocks on a local machine is part of this concept. We will look at this and Proof of Work again in later sections.

The way this is achieved is by using two values present inside each block: the nonce and the difficulty target.

The nonce

This is a randomly generated number. The reason it is here is so that one can add different nonce values, and when hashed with the block we will get different hashes as a result. We can generate many different hashes by varying the nonce. As we know, hashes are numbers, even if they don't always appear so when being presented as hexadecimal.

The Difficulty Target

This is a value that the hash of the block that we want to add, including the nonce, has to be below for the next block to be valid. The Difficulty Target for this block is listed in the previous block.

So, say we have a Difficulty Target of 10 and the hash function can produce numbers up to 100. The actual numbers are likely to be a great deal larger than this, but for the sake of simplicity, let's use this as our example.

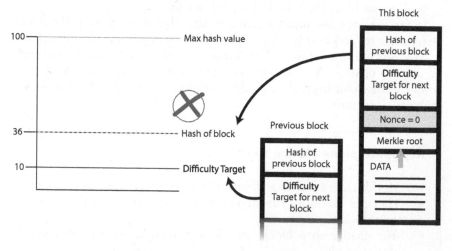

Figure 2.19 Difficulty Target.

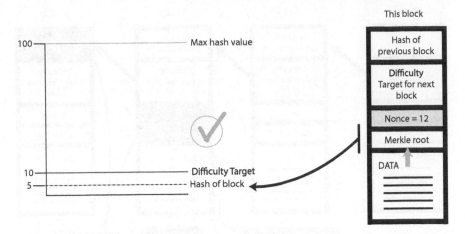

Figure 2.20 Difficulty Target reached.

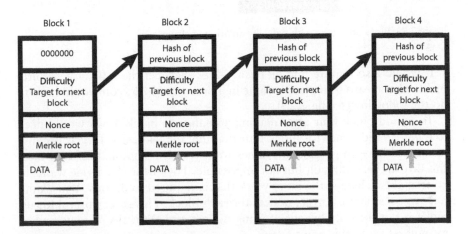

Figure 2.21 Block structure with difficulty and nonce.

The hash of the next block needs to be below this. The system trying to add the next block might try hashing with a nonce of 0.

That creates a hash of 36. That was not below our target and so it generates a new nonce and tries again. It will do this repeatedly until it can find a value that is below the Difficulty Target (fig 2.20).

So now we have a block that looks like this:

With the structure we have developed (fig 2.21) it is difficult to change any given value in a previous block because this would invalidate the hashes in the block that was changed and the following blocks, as highlighted here:

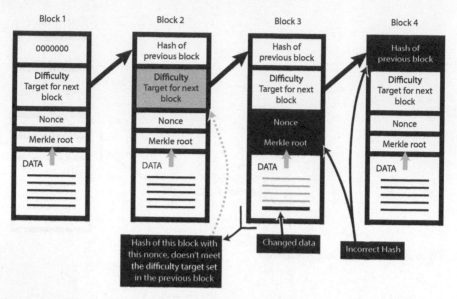

Figure 2.22 Block structure with difficulty and nonce changes.

It would also require finding hash values that met the difficulty requirement. That means to replace a value in a previous block, you would have to do the following (see fig 2.23).

To re-add block four after making a change to block 3, we would need to guess a valid nonce for block four that met the Difficulty Target. Because we would have to guess many times to generate a suitable nonce to meet this target, this is difficult but not impossible. The further back one wants to go to make a change, the more work that is required to do this. You would have to guess at the correct nonces for each block. This is very useful for us, but it is not the only benefit of using nonces and Difficulty Targets and so we will return to this point again.

Note: You may ask why the user would not just set themselves a Difficulty Target that was easy to attain. We will look at why this is not possible when we revisit Difficulty Targets later.

The blockchain we have created so far is theoretically at least on just one computer. This makes it possible to change the whole chain and so the next weakness that we will address is that of centralization. To resolve this, we need to explore distribution across a network. Before we move on though,

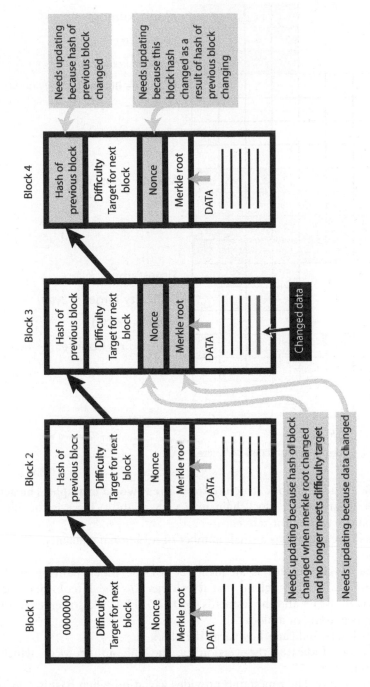

Figure 2.23 Block structure with difficulty and nonce changes to correct.

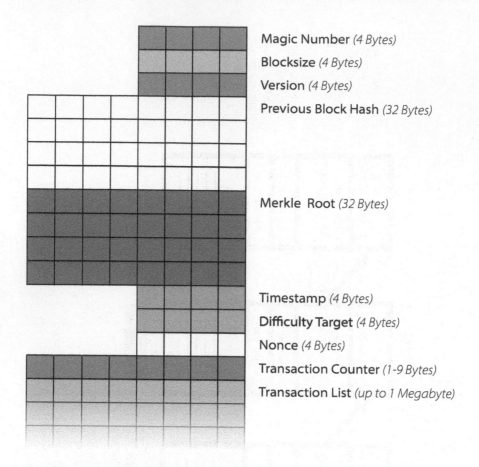

Figure 2.24 Bitcoin block structure complete.

let's look at the full block structure from a real-world example. The actual structure in any given blockchain may vary slightly. Here is the Bitcoin blockchain structure, for reference.

You will see that it has a small number of additional elements.

- The Magic number is an identifier for the Blockchain network. It identifies the blockchain that it belongs to. The Bitcoin main-net is 0xD9B4BEF9 and the testnet is 0xDAB5BFFA. It also serves to mark the beginning of a block.
- Block size: Indicates how large the block is.
- Version: Indicates the version of the Bitcoin protocol which is being used.
- Timestamp: The timestamp provides variation when hashing, as well as a method for additional validation.

Block	
Hash	000000000000000000010768d91b882ecc9abec437b09866d9ab6129955fce10d
Confirmations	63,699
Timestamp	2020-05-06 17:10
Number of transactions	2,177
Difficulty	16,104,807,485,529.38
Merkle root	d6ae699fee699b29f28370c6ad158e75a869c62ea1de512fdd6e38a3722bf207
Version	0x20c00000
Bits	387,021,369
Weight	3,992,902 WU
Size	1,258,837 bytes
Nonce	1,399,553,976
Transaction volume	4948.86581112 BTC
Block reward	12.50000000 BTC
Fee reward	0.43301495 BTC

Figure 2.25 Block from the Bitcoin network.

- Transaction Counter: This lists the number of transactions that are included with the block.
- Transaction List: This contains the transaction data in the block. We will look more at the transaction structure later in the book.

Let's have a look at some actual Bitcoin blocks in Figure 2.25.

You can see many of the values that we have discussed and some we haven't. Some of these relate to the information stored in the block and others describe the block. Don't worry if there is information there that you are not familiar with. We have a lot left to look at! See how the hash of the block starts with many zeros? This is because the hash of the block must be lower to meet the Difficulty Target. The nonce that allowed it to meet that target was 1,399,553,976. Though there will have been other valid nonces that would have resulted in hashes that also met the Difficulty Target.

Key points about difficulty and nonces

- The block's data is hashed to create a value.
- The block has a value called nonce which can be changed to change the resultant hash.
- There is a Difficulty Target value which the hash of the block must be below to be accepted.
- This makes it difficult to create a block, which helps to protect against the blockchain being rewritten afterwards.

Chapter 3

Decentralized computing

Blockchains are typically distributed across a network. They communicate with each other over the internet. The nodes on the network maintain a copy of the blockchain which they can read and verify (fig 3.1).

The nodes can compare their copy of the blockchain with the copy on the other nodes. This allows them to update each other. If they find that the node they are checking with has a different copy of the blockchain, then whichever node has the longest chain will win out and both nodes will switch to the longest version. The number of blocks in the blockchain is referred to as the block height.

By switching to the highest block height, the network ensures that it is always investing in the version of the blockchain that has had the most work done to it as it takes time and power run the machines to guess nonces and generate a valid hash. The work taken to produce a block can be considerable. This mechanism of using hash power to establish work done is called *Proof of Work*. If we assume that the majority of nodes are "honest", this is a mechanism for securing the system. We will look at this again in more detail later.

Blockchains operate by consensus, according to the protocol for that particular blockchain. The nodes on the network come to a consensus about the validity of the blocks and the chain which is formed from them. They agree on one version of the truth; one version of the chain.

Nodes can be full nodes or partial nodes. If a node containing only a partial chain needs to look up data that it does not have itself, it can consult a full node for the additional information. When you discuss blockchains, you will quickly come across the term "miner". Normally nodes in the blockchain only hold the information, read, verify and distribute the chain. Miners are nodes that can write to the chain. We will revisit this later when we talk about cryptocurrencies.

Let's look at an example. In this example, one of the nodes has created a new block. It is passed along to the next nodes (fig 3.2).

DOI: 10.1201/9781003187165-3

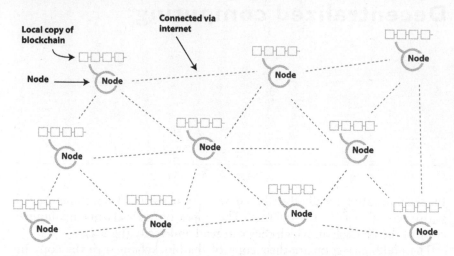

Figure 3.1 Blockchain network.

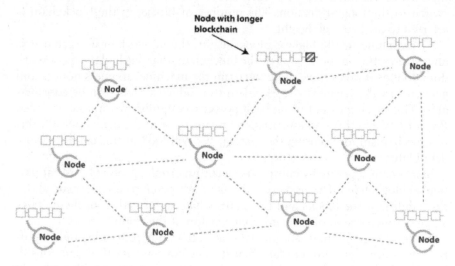

Figure 3.2 A block is added.

This is then passed to the surrounding nodes (fig 3.3).

Until it has made its way across the network (fig 3.4).

This means that it is practically impossible to go in and change a single value. Let's run through an example of what would happen if someone tried to do that.

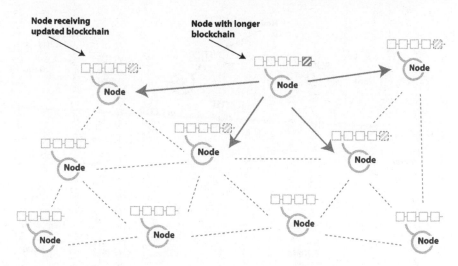

Figure 3.3 Nodes sending chain.

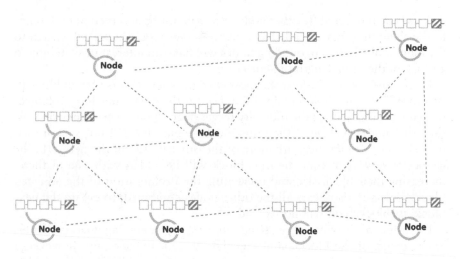

Figure 3.4 All nodes updated.

Say the darker node "Node A" tried to change a value in block number two. As we have seen, that would invalidate that block and the following blocks. Let's assume it has re-calculated the Merkle tree and the nonce so that it has recreated its own block two. The blockchain height is reduced for that copy of the blockchain.

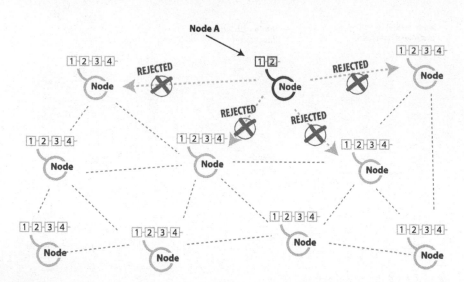

Figure 3.5 Nodes rejecting shorter chain.

This is then rejected by other nodes and will not be accepted in preference to the chain that they already have. As we know, blockchains will switch to the longest block, so surrounding nodes will have no interest in switching to a block of the same length or shorter.

Even if they try and adjust the most current block, this is very unlikely to succeed. They must first find a valid nonce for the block they have changed, to make the block meet the difficulty target once again. Even if they do this, the other nodes will be at the same block height and will not switch to it in preference. While there are more of the other nodes on the network, the chance is very great that the next block will be added with one of them, increasing their block size and preventing the proliferation of the adjusted block. Unless it also beats all the other nodes combined, to create the next block, its blockchain will not spread.

By using a distributed system, we are protecting against malicious amendments of the blockchain after data is added. There are, however, a few other benefits of using a distributed approach. In addition, it also makes it very difficult to stop the network. With a centralized service, it is relatively easy to take down the whole system. Say, for example, laws in the country the server resides in makes it illegal to provide such a service, the whole system can be stopped with relative ease (fig 3.6).

Maybe the system is attacked either physically or with a cyber-attack. Such an attack would have a much more difficult task, given that one could take down several nodes and the system would still function (fig 3.7).

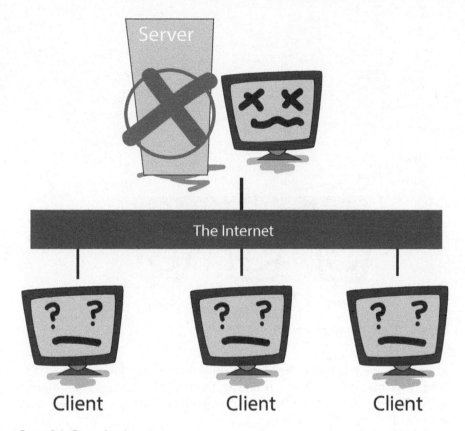

Figure 3.6 Centralized service.

Note: Satoshi Nakamoto (2008) said "Governments are good at cutting off the heads of a centrally controlled networks like Napster, but pure P2P networks like Gnutella and Tor seem to be holding their own."

In such a scenario, the network would continue to function. If and when the attacked nodes returned to the network, they would compare any chain they might still have stored and find that the new chain had carried on growing, would update themselves and carry on as normal. At this stage, it would be extremely difficult to remove a well-established blockchain from existence by force.

What does this mean? We don't need to trust in people to do what they say, we trust the system. For supply chains we don't need to trust the origin

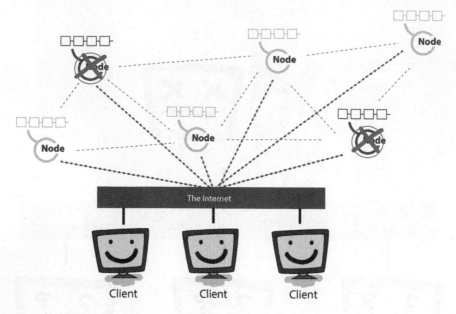

Figure 3.7 Decentralized service.

of an item, we can check the blockchain, secure in the knowledge that so long as the majority of nodes are honest, then the blockchain is untampered with. For finance, we don't need to trust banks to manage our assets, they are managed by the blockchain.

PARTIAL NODES

The kinds of nodes that we have discussed so far are sometimes referred to as *full nodes*. That is to say that they have a local copy of the full blockchain. Blockchains can grow quite sizeable. The Bitcoin blockchain is around 350 gigabytes at the time of writing this. Holding a full copy of the blockchain is not reasonable in many circumstances. It is also possible, therefore, to have *partial nodes*. These are nodes that hold only a section of the blockchain. If they need to refer to information in a block they are not holding, then they can refer to a full node on the network.

Summary of the blockchain so far.

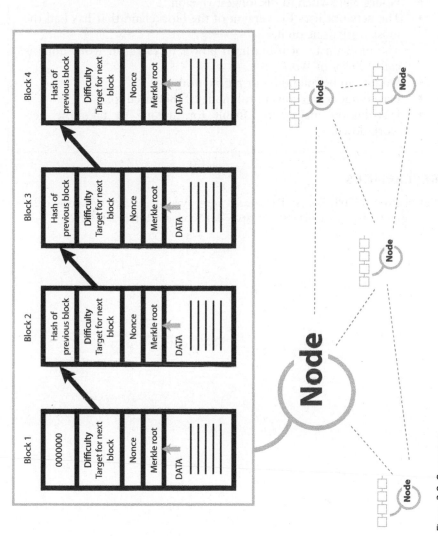

Figure 3.8 Summary.

Key points about nodes and networks

- The nodes can compare their copy of the blockchain with the copy on the other nodes.
- Nodes will switch to the longest version.
- The network uses the version of the blockchain that has had the most work done on it.
- The mechanism of using hash power to establish work done is called *Proof of Work*.
- Nodes can be full nodes or partial nodes.
- Partial nodes can consult full nodes if they need to.
- Distribution makes it difficult for anyone to take the network down.

REFERENCES

Nakamoto, S. (2008) *Bitcoin P2P e-cash paper* Available at https://satoshi.nakamo toinstitute.org/emails/cryptography/4/ [Accessed 29 July 2021].

Chapter 4

Forks

When there are different versions of the blockchain in existence at the same time, we call this a fork. There are two main reasons why this might happen: accidentally and through an update. Let's look at accidental forks first.

ACCIDENTAL FORKS

Consider this situation. We have a blockchain network, currently, the block height is 4 and the systems on the network are busy generating new nonces and hashing the block so that they can add it to the system (fig 4.1).

A suitable nonce is found at node A that creates a hash that meets the Difficulty Target and so a new block is created. It then begins propagating it to the systems around it. Naturally, it will normally propagate more quickly to the systems nearest to it. They compare their chain and see that the one held by A has a higher block height of 5 and so update themselves (fig 4.2).

Now imagine before it can receive the update, a new nonce and suitable hash is found that meets the Difficulty Target at node B. It also begins updating the nodes around it (fig 4.3).

We now have two versions of the blockchain that are maintained simultaneously, by different machines (fig 4.4).

The solid block nodes consider the bottom blockchain to be the version of the truth, the stripey block systems consider the top blockchain to be the truth (fig 4.5).

This is what we call an accidental fork and they occur with some regularity. It's not as much of a problem as it might sound. At this stage, because all nodes contain blockchains with the same block height and both chains are valid, they will not update from each other and we remain at a stalemate, at least for now.

These forks will, however, resolve themselves. When block 6 is created, it will again begin to propagate and all the systems around it will update themselves with the longest blockchain (fig 4.6).

DOI: 10.1201/9781003187165-4

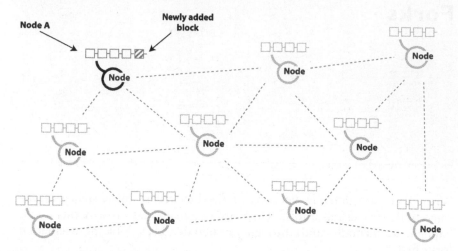

Figure 4.1 Newly mined block.

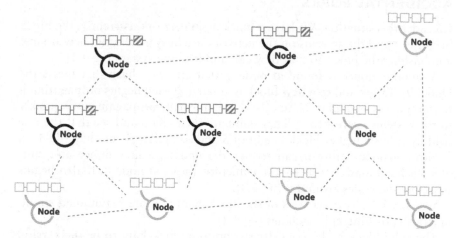

Figure 4.2 Block distribution.

Normally the blockchain held by the systems with the highest hash power will win out and become the one version of the truth as they are more likely to find the next block and add it to the chain. This is why we wait for confirmations before we consider the data to be set (fig 4.7).

Confirmations are the number of blocks added to the chain after the one that includes your information. The larger the number of confirmations, the less likely it is that that data is changed in the future. Forking and the fact that data is more difficult to change when it has more blocks following it is

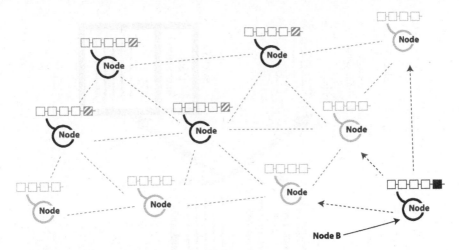

Figure 4.3 A different new block.

the reason why we wait for confirmations. We do not know whether there are other machines on the network that have a different blockchain and our block might be part of a fork. The more confirmed blocks, the less likely this is to be the case. Figure 4.8 shows how likely it is that a block remains in a fork at progressive levels of confirmation.

At this point, it is highly unlikely that there is a fork that has not resolved and so we can consider it to be set by the system. You will sometimes hear of systems requiring different numbers of confirmations before they are satisfied that it has been irreversibly written onto the blockchain.

When an accidental fork resolves itself, the block that fails to make it into the block is called an orphaned block, or a stale block. The data from it is not written into the blockchain at this point. That isn't to say that it will never be written into the blockchain, just that it has not made it into the chain in that particular block. We will discuss what happens to the data in a stale block in a little more detail later on.

We have discussed difficulty, nonces and the hashing of blocks to meet the Difficulty Target. The difficulty value is not set however, it can be varied, according to the amount of hash power on the network (fig 4.9).

When there are lots of systems on the network, or as the processing speed of those machines increases, the speed with which they can generate nonces, hash the block and check it against the Difficulty Target increases (fig 4.10).

This will mean that blocks are created more quickly. This creates a few problems. It means that potentially we are creating more blocks than we need to contain the data, which is wasteful. It also increases the chance of creating a stale block.

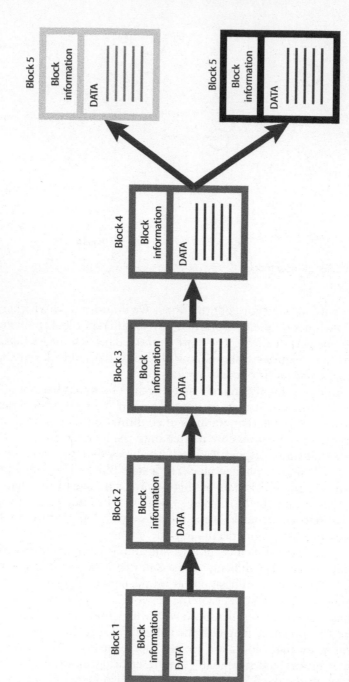

Figure 4.4 Forked chain.

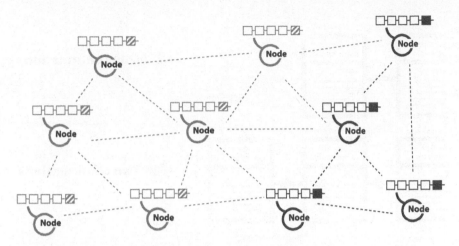

Figure 4.5 Nodes with different blocks.

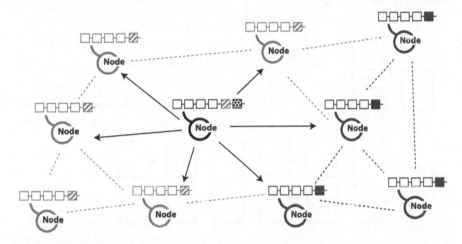

Figure 4.6 Another block is added.

To address this, the difficulty is increased when the hash power goes up in order to keep block creations separated in time sufficiently to allow new blocks to propagate before another block is produced. This reduces the instances of accidental forks.

Example

Imagine that the maximum possible value for the hash is 1000. In actuality, this value is orders of magnitude higher, but for this simple example, we will stick to 1000. We divide this by the difficulty to get the Difficulty Target.

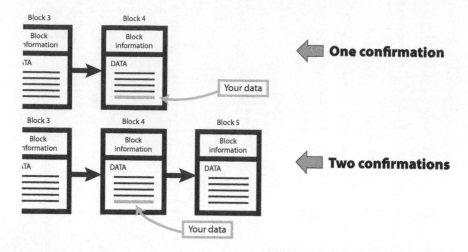

Figure 4.7 Confirmations.

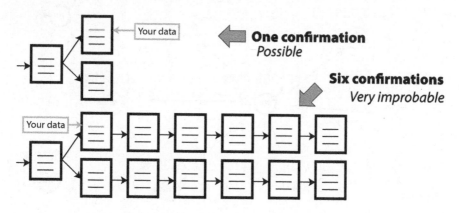

Figure 4.8 Forking probabilities.

In this example, the difficulty is set at 2. This means that the hash of the next block must be lower than or equal to 500 (fig 4.12).

By dividing the maximum possible hash value by the difficulty, we have an easy method of controlling the Difficulty Target. The equation to calculate the Difficulty Target is

$$DifficultyTarget = \frac{Maximum\,Hash\,Value}{Difficulty}$$

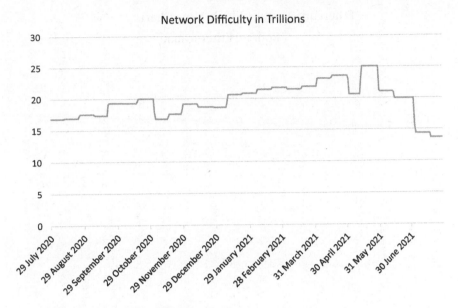

Figure 4.9 Bitcoin networks difficulty over time.

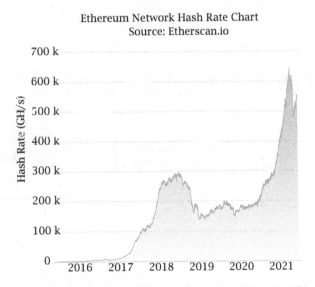

Figure 4.10 The hash rate of the Ethereum blockchain network over time (Etherscan 2021). Excerpt from Etherscan.io available at https://etherscan.io/chart/hashrate

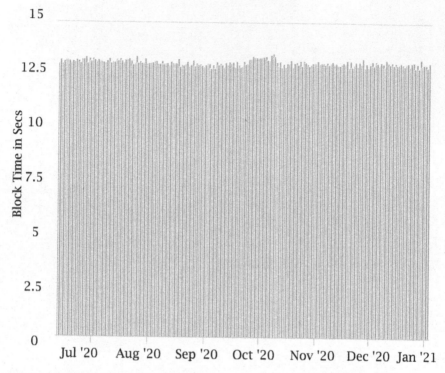

Ethereum Average Block Time Chart
Source: Etherscan.io

Figure 4.11 The block time of a cryptocurrency over time (Etherscan 2021B).
Excerpt from Etherscan.io available at https://etherscan.io/chart/blocktime

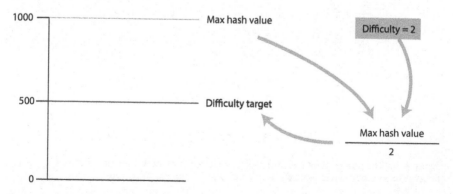

Figure 4.12 Variable Difficulty Target.

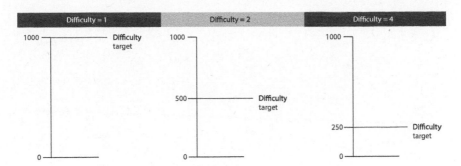

Figure 4.13 Different Difficulty Targets.

When the difficulty value goes up, the target goes down (fig 4.13).

With this mechanism we can adjust the difficulty, in response to the overall hash rate of the network and the changes in block time, to keep the block time to a reasonable value. When the difficulty is high, the target is low and when the difficulty is low, the target is high.

 Note: The Bitcoin difficulty is adjusted every 2016 blocks.

UPDATE FORK

When there is an update to a blockchain network, if all systems on the network do not receive the update, it can cause a fork. This happens when nodes on the network have different rules for what constitutes a valid block.

There are a couple of different types of fork that result from this type of change. To explore them, let's consider an example. In this example we start with a network of nodes, happily working on a blockchain with 1 mb maximum allowable block size. They have just finished working on block 3, it is added to the chain and distributed around the network (fig 4.14).

Now let's consider what might happen if the community of developers for a particular blockchain decided to create an update that reduced the maximum block size. Let's say it is reduced to 0.5 mb. If everyone updated, then this would not cause any issues, the chain would continue as normal. Unfortunately, not everyone on the network could agree about this update and so some systems do not update. In the diagram, updated systems are shown in a darker shade and un-updated systems are shown in a lighter shade (fig 4.15).

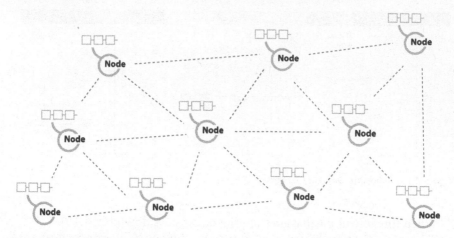

Figure 4.14 A blockchain network.

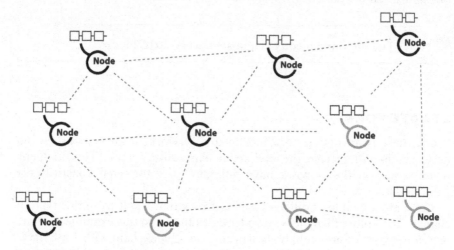

Figure 4.15 Some nodes update.

Let's say a new block is created at node A. This updated blockchain is shown in diagonal stripes. Node A has been updated and so it creates a block that is 0.5 mb or less (fig 4.16).

This is accepted across the network and so this version of the block is distributed across the network (fig 4.17).

Now let's say the next block is created at point B, this time it is shown with spots (fig 4.18).

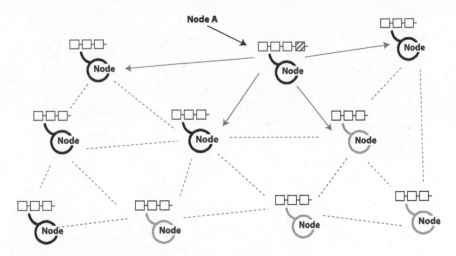

Figure 4.16 A new block is added.

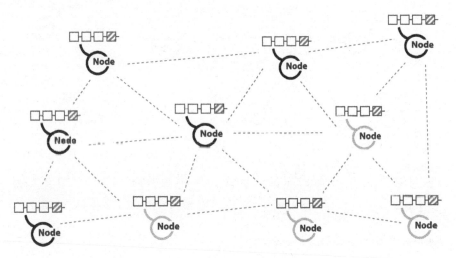

Figure 4.17 Block accepted.

Node B does not have the update and so it will typically create a block larger than 0.5 mb. This is accepted by other un-updated systems, but when updated systems check this version, they find it to be invalid and so will not add it (fig 4.19).

As the darker updated nodes outnumber and out-hash power the lighter un-updated nodes, they will generate more new blocks than them. This

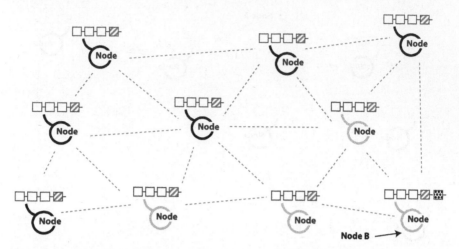

Figure 4.18 Node B's new block.

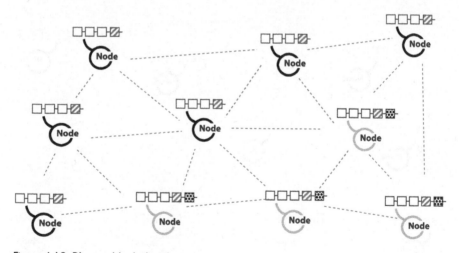

Figure 4.19 B's new block distributes.

means that their chain will grow faster, be accepted by all nodes and their version of the blockchain will win-out.

SOFT FORK

The kind of fork we have just described is known as a *soft fork*. This is the term given to an update that makes previously valid blocks invalid. That is to say that they implement a restriction of the rules. Features of a soft fork are that the network will continue as normal, but from that point, the lighter un-updated nodes will be unable to add any blocks to the network. This is good for limiting the disruption caused by differences in opinion on the development of the blockchain, but not so great if you didn't agree to the update and are effectively having the choice forced upon you.

HARD FORK

The other type of fork, unsurprisingly, is a hard fork. Conversely, it reduces restrictions, making previously invalid blocks valid. Let's look at an example. Imagine rather than halving the maximum allowable block size, we double it so that updated nodes can accept blocks of 2 mb. We will again use dark shading for updated systems and light shading for un-updated systems.

Let's say that a new block of 2 mb is created at point A. This is again shown in stripes. It is distributed across the network, but this time it will not be accepted by the un-updated lighter nodes (fig 4.20).

Now let's consider what would happen if a new block were created in the lighter un-updated nodes. That would be distributed across the lighter un-updated network, and though its blocks are valid on the updated network, its blocks will never be used on the updated system, because it is not longer than the chain they already have.

The darker updated nodes will create the longest chain as they have more hash power, but it will never be accepted by the lighter un-updated nodes. They instead will carry on working on the chain that they have. In effect this creates two different blockchains, each maintaining their own version. There are several instances of this happening over the past years.

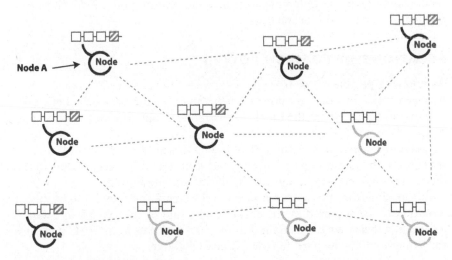

Figure 4.20 Node A's new block.

Note: Bitcoin Cash and Bitcoin SV were created from the result of a disagreement over block size which resulted in a hard fork

You can see from the two examples above:

- Soft forks
  - Result from a restriction of the criteria, making blocks that were previously valid invalid, such as reducing the maximum allowable block size.
  - Result in un-updated nodes effectively no longer being able to write to the blockchain.
- Hard forks
  - Result from a loosening of the criteria, making blocks that were previous invalid, become valid, such as increasing the maximum allowable block size.
  - Result in un-updated nodes effectively maintaining their own blockchain.

Both fork types reduce the hash power on the network as they reduce the number of systems generating hashes that create new blocks. With soft forks, this is a result of the blocks created by the lighter systems being repeatedly orphaned. With the hard fork, this is as a result of the two blockchains splitting the hash power between them. In these situations, it is not only the hash power that is divided. Often the community is split too, with developers insistent on their direction for the development of the blockchain moving in different directions and working on the development of the now separated blockchains.

RELATIONSHIP TO HASH POWER

As you may be able to see from the examples above, there is a relationship between forks and the amount of hash power on the network. Let's take our first example where the block size is reduced but consider what would happen if only a few systems updated (fig 4.21).

Imagine a block was created at point A. It would be 1 mb in size as it was created by an un-updated system and so it would be accepted by all the lighter un-updated nodes, but not the darker updated nodes.

In this situation, the lighter nodes would create the longer chain, but it would never be accepted by the darker nodes and so the two groups would be creating their own blockchain. Rather than acting as a soft fork, it creates the same result as the hard fork we discussed above.

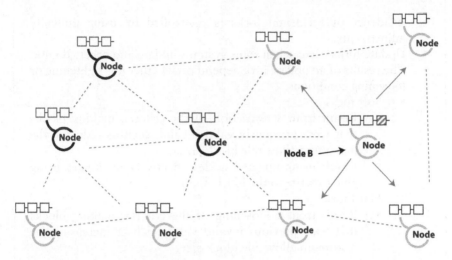

Figure 4.21 New block for node A.

Equally, if we consider the hard fork example where the maximum block size is increased to 2 mb, but this time where only a few systems update, we can see that a new block created with the majority of un-updated nodes will be distributed all across the network. New blocks made in the small number of updated systems will not be accepted by the un-updated nodes.

Given that the un-updated nodes outnumber them, they will not be able to compete with the increased hash power of the larger network and ultimately their version of the blockchain will win-out, creating the same as a soft fork.

Generally speaking, though, updates are not typically rolled out without majority approval and implementation, so the general rule that soft forks are less disruptive and hard forks split the network will hold true.

You can probably see from the examples above that any soft forking will increase the occurrence of stale blocks.

Key points about forks

- Accidental forks are caused when new blocks are found in multiple places on the network before one version can be fully distributed across the network.
- Accidental forks will resolve themselves when one chain grows longer.
- Accidental forks are affected by block time.

- Incidence of accidental forks is controlled by using difficulty adjustments.
- Update forks occur when some systems update and others do not.
- The results of an update fork depend on whether it is tightening or loosening conditions.
  - Soft forks
    - Result from a restriction of the criteria, making blocks that were previously valid invalid, such as reducing the maximum allowable block size.
    - Result in un-updated nodes effectively no longer being able to write to the blockchain.
  - Hard forks
    - Result from a loosening of the criteria, making blocks that were previous invalid valid, such as increasing the maximum allowable block size.

REFERENCES

Etherscan (2021) *Ethereum Network Hash Rate Chart* Available from https://etherscan.io/chart/hashrate [Accessed 29 July 2021].

Etherscan (2021 B) *Ethereum Average Block Time Chart* Available from https://etherscan.io/chart/blocktime [Accessed 29 July 2021].

Chapter 5

Cryptocurrencies

Blockchains were first created for use in cryptocurrencies. The very first blockchain was proposed in a white paper, "Bitcoin: A Peer-to-Peer Electronic Cash System" by Satoshi Nakamoto, in 2008. Blockchains provide a great solution to the management of digital assets because of their immutable nature and their resilience to attack.

Though initially there was only Bitcoin, the code for it is open source and many additional cryptocurrencies have been created. The use of open-source code is important for the users of the system to trust in it and to allow developers to form communities and continue to work on it.

Cryptocurrencies extend what we have already learned about blockchains with additional rules specifically related to asset-based transactions. The data that they contain in the blocks relate to these transactions. They also involve the use of wallets, exchanges and miners. They offer additional rules for how and when to do things. We will look at each of these and plenty more in the coming section.

We will be looking through Bitcoin as an example. But the same principles generally apply to other cryptocurrencies.

WHAT ARE THE BENEFITS OF CRYPTOCURRENCIES?

Fees

They reduce the fees that one must pay to transact. Because, as we have discussed, transactions are paid based on how much size they take up, rather than how much money you transfer, they can significantly reduce the cost of transnational transactions.

Control

When you hold money in a bank, they control your assets. They can and frequently do tell you what you are allowed to spend your money on and who you are allowed to send it to. They can freeze your account and limit

DOI: 10.1201/9781003187165-5

your access to your assets. They take the assets and lend them out to others in the form of loans and mortgages.

With cryptocurrencies, you are in control of your assets. No bank, government or other entity can restrict your access to your funds. If you hold the funds, then you alone can decide where and when to transfer them. You can also lend your assets out and earn interest for doing so, without the need of a bank.

More confidential transactions

Under cash/credit systems, your entire transaction history may become a reference document for the bank or credit agency involved, each time you make a transaction. At the simplest level, this might involve a check on your account balances, to ensure that sufficient funds are available. For more complex or business-critical transactions, a more thorough examination of your financial history might be required.

Protection against fraud

Identity theft is an issue for the traditional banking system, where one only needs to create fake bills and ID to gain access to someone's account. Cryptocurrencies protect against this by using a system of keys that we will look at in the coming section.

Secure

Banks and financial services gather many people's wealth into a single area. This can make a very tempting target for hackers. By keeping your wealth individually, anyone who wanted to gain access to this would have to individually gain access to each wallet.

Flexible

Cryptocurrencies are essentially programs running on a distributed network. They can be programmed to have all sorts of attributes. Many cryptocurrencies have been made for a wide variety of different purposes, some to automate the transfer of funds, some to provide high levels of privacy. They are very flexible in their uses.

Transparency

In cryptocurrency, every transaction recorded on the blockchain. All information is only added to and never removed. When an address is used to move assets, it is publicly visible. It is not immediately obvious who owns the address, however. This makes activities like auditing more transparent and easier to perform.

Easy to carry

Rather than carrying large amounts of cash or assets with you when you travel, cryptocurrencies can be transported on your phone, on a small device or even just by remembering a key phrase.

WHAT ARE WALLETS?

One key feature of cryptocurrencies is their use of wallets. These can be compared to the wallets and purses that one might store their fiat currencies in, in coins and notes. They do not, however, store anything in them, they are more a mechanism for tracking the assets that you have in the blockchain and creating transactions to be stored on the blockchain.

There are different types of wallet and we will look at these, but let's first look at how a basic wallet functions. Wallets are, in their most basic form, a private key used for encryption. To understand how they work, we need to know a little about encryption, so let's start there. We will begin by looking at basic encryption and then move on to the type of encryption that is used in cryptocurrency wallets called public/private key encryption.

Although learning a little about encryption is not as challenging as you might think, it is possible to have a more general understanding of blockchains if you can accept the key principles of public/private key encryption. For this reason, it would be acceptable to move to the "key points" part at the end of the encryption section.

ENCRYPTION

In encryption, a *key* is used to effectively encode data, so when a piece of data is entered, an unrecognizable piece of data is outputted. You will then need a key to decode it again. With some types of encryption, it is the same key that encrypts and decrypts the data, this is called a reciprocal. With others, it is a separate key and this is non-reciprocal.

You will probably be familiar with some encryption already, possibly you have made a code when you were a child, by shifting numbers of the alphabet along, like this example where each character is shifted five places (fig 5.1).

If we consider this process to be our encryption process, we would expect the following outputs for the following inputs (fig 5.2).

This would be an example of a non-reciprocal key. This means that you do not get the original text by reapplying the key. We would have to use a shift of -5 to decode. Though, given that there are 26 letters in the alphabet, we could make this reciprocal by shifting 13 places (fig 5.3).

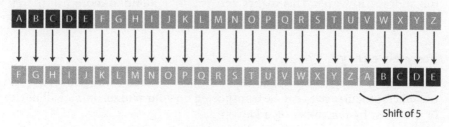

Figure 5.1 Shift of five.

Figure 5.2 Shift of five encryption.

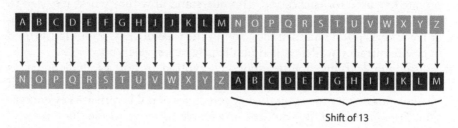

Figure 5.3 Shift of thirteen.

SHARED KEY ENCRYPTION

With shared key encryption, the encoding and the decoding may use the same key. Sometimes that key is reciprocal and the same function will decode the message and sometimes it requires switching to a different mode.

Both of the shifting codes that we used above would fall into this category. To encode and decode a message, both the sender, let's call them Jill, and receiver, let's call him Jack, would need to share the key (fig 5.4).

They could then encrypt using the shared key of 5 or decrypt by using the negative of the key, -5. If someone were to be viewing that message, then they would only see the encrypted message and, in principle at least, not be able to understand it (fig 5.5).

Jack and Jill, however, would be able to decode and understand the message. An important limitation of shared key encryption is that to be

Figure 5.4 Shared key.

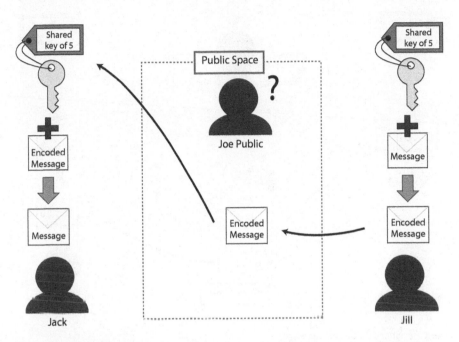

Figure 5.5 Sharing key.

able to share messages, one must first agree on a key. If that agreement is intercepted at that time, the messages are not secure (fig 5.6).

Here the key is being intercepted by Joe Public and he is now able to decrypt any communications between Jack and Jill.

The only way of sending a secure message is to encrypt it and the only method of creating an encryption channel is to have a secured key. You can probably see the problem here. In the real world, it is probably quite easy to find a secure method of exchanging keys, but in an age where everything is connected, shared key encryption offers little protection to us for most applications.

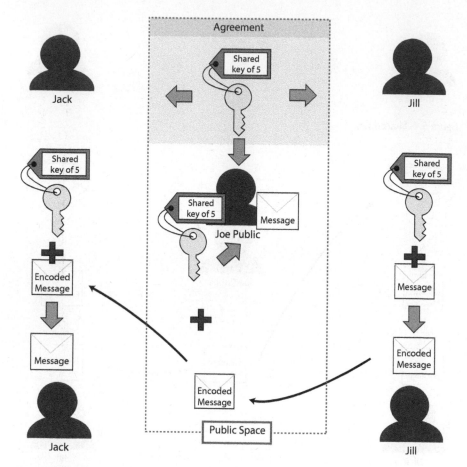

Figure 5.6 Sharing key and message.

ASYMMETRIC ENCRYPTION

This method of encryption uses a pair of key codes. Much like our alphabet shifting where we could encode with 5 and decode with -5, one key will encode the data that the other key will decode. In just the same manner, they will each decode what the other one codes (fig 5.7).

Unlike the alphabet shifting example, however, where we could simply negate the shift from 5 to -5, it is not easy to work out one key from the other.

A very large random value is used to create the two keys. One of these will be kept private and the other will be made public (fig 5.8).

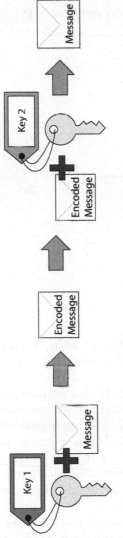

Figure 5.7 Asymmetric encryption with two keys.

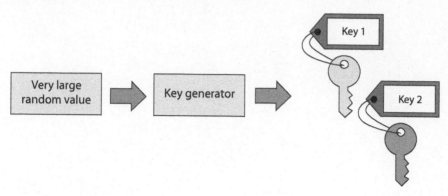

Figure 5.8 Key generator.

Figure 5.9 Key generation phase.

Because each key will decrypt what the other key encrypts, it is not important which of the keys is made public only that one of the keys is kept securely.

Let's look at an example. In this example, Jack and Jill want to share messages securely. We will consider all communication to be public, as we cannot guarantee it is secure. They each generate a key pair (fig 5.9).

Then they share their keys. This is shown in the Figure 5.10. Starting with the key generators, we can see that they share their public keys available to each other by making them public. Joe public will also receive them. To follow the path of sharing, start at the key generators and follow the sharing for each key.

If Jill wants to send a message to Jack, she takes Jack's public key and encrypts the message with it and sends it (fig 5.11).

The message is then taken by John and he uses the key that he kept private to decode the message. Using this method, if the messages are intercepted, the interceptor does not have the private keys with which to decode the message.

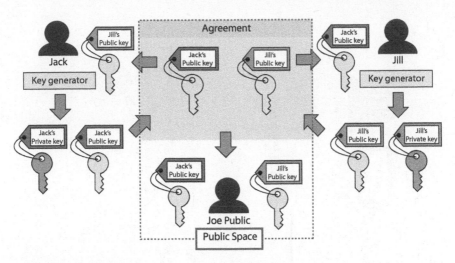

Figure 5.10 Agreement phase.

SIGNATURES

Another key function of public and private keys is the ability to "sign" information to show that you were the originator. In this case, let's assume that John isn't sending sensitive information, but just needs Jane to know that it was sent by him.

In the example in figure 5.12 Jack takes the data and uses his private key to sign it. Jill and any other person who intercepts the message can use Jack's public key to check the signature and will be able to tell that Jack must have sent it, as only Jack holds the private key that encodes for his public key.

Because it was made with his private key, anyone, not just the unintended recipient with his public key, can confirm that it was Jack that sent the message. We can use this method, combined with the one above to securely encode and sign a message.

In the example shown in figure 5.13, Jill wants to send a secret message to Jack, ensure he knows it is from her. To do this she

1. Takes the message and encrypts it using Jack's public key.
2. Takes they encrypted message and signs it using her private key.

When Jack receives the message, he needs to verify the sender and decode the message. To this he

1. He checks the signature is decodable using Jill's public key to ensure it was made by Jill.
2. Then he decodes the message using his private key.

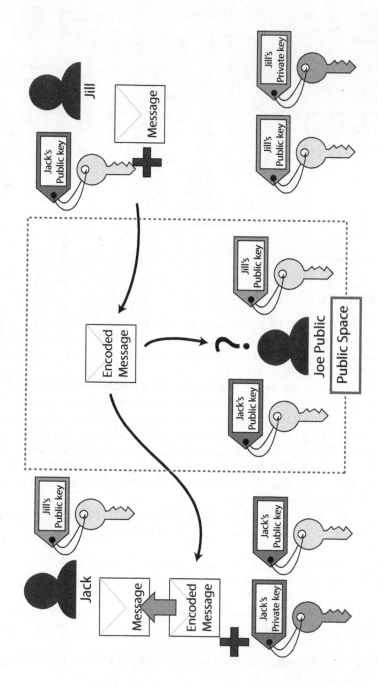

Figure 5.11 Messaging.

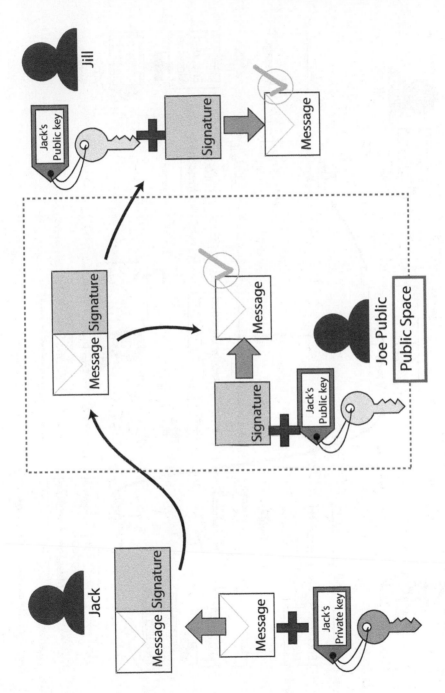

Figure 5.12 Signed message.

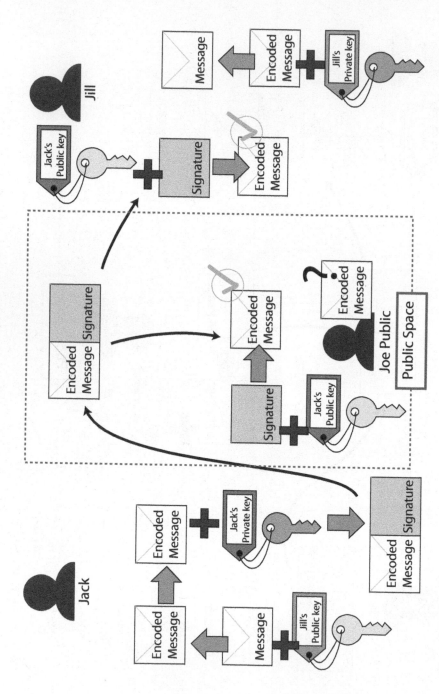

Figure 5.13 Signed encoded message.

Note: Public and private key encryption can be quite slow when compared to shared key encryption. For this reason, it is common to use public/private key encryption to share a shared key code and then move to shared key methods.

These are the general principles of encryption and this provides a reasonable working overview of all you need to understand to work with cryptocurrencies. If, however, you want to understand in more detail exactly what is happening, we need to talk about Elliptic Curve Cryptography, which we will look at next.

Note: Cryptography literally means secret writing.

Key points about encryption

- Public and private keys are numerical codes or representations of numerical codes that are used to encrypt data.
- Private keys need to be kept secure.
- Public keys are shared.
- It is not reasonably possible to work out the private key from the public key.
- Private keys can be used to create a digital signature that shows who created it.

ELLIPTIC CURVE CRYPTOGRAPHY

The foundation of cryptography used in cryptocurrency is based on Elliptic Curve Cryptography or ECC. It is also known as Elliptic Curve Digital Signature Algorithm or ECDSA. The principle may take a little concentration to understand and so I will try and take this very slowly. It is, however, quite possible to understand more generally how cryptocurrencies work without understanding what is happening with ECC, so if you struggle with this section and have tried reading it a couple of times, feel free to skip to the key points and continue.

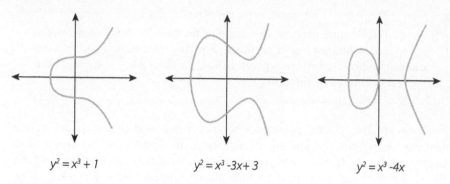

$y^2 = x^3 + 1$ $y^2 = x^3 - 3x + 3$ $y^2 = x^3 - 4x$

Figure 5.14 Different elliptic curve graphs.

With ECC you start with an elliptic curve, which results from some form of the formula:

$$y^2 = x^3 + ax + b$$

So, we can plot a graph of this. By square rooting both sides we get:

$$y = \pm\sqrt{x^3 + ax + b}$$

The values of "a" and "b" can be changed to create different graphs.

The elliptic curve used by Bitcoin is secp256k1. The equation for the secp256k1 curve is $y^2 = x^3 + 7$ This curve is approximated in the graph shown in figure 5.15.

The principle works on the basis of adding two points together. So, let us start with point 1 (*1.P*) and point 2 (*2.P*) shown in figure 5.16.

To work out point 3.*P* we would draw a line between our two points (fig 5.17)

Look for the third intersection of the line between them (fig 5.18)

Then we flip it to the other side, as shown in figure 5.19.

So 1.*P* + 2.*P* = 3.*P*

If we do it again, we will get 4.*P* then 5.*P* and so on.

To start, we can either use two set points or we can begin with just one point P. If we are starting with one point, to create 2.*P*, we will need to use the tangent of the first point, as we do not have two separate points with which to create the line (fig 5.20).

This will give us our second point 2.*P* and we can continue from there as before (fig 5.21).

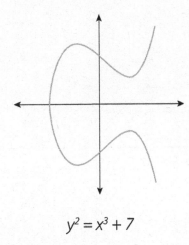

$$y^2 = x^3 + 7$$

Figure 5.15 The Bitcoin elliptic curve.

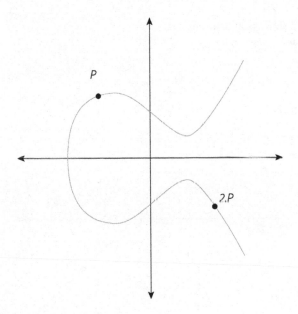

Figure 5.16 EC showing two points.

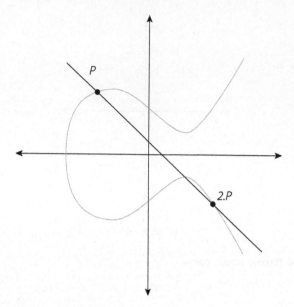

Figure 5.17 EC showing intersecting line.

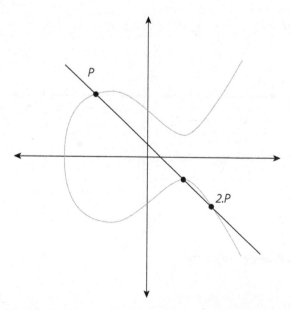

Figure 5.18 Third point.

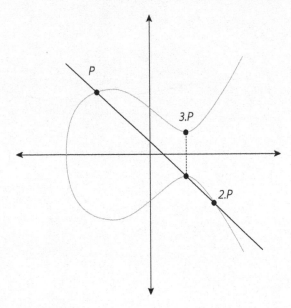

Figure 5.19 Flipped point.

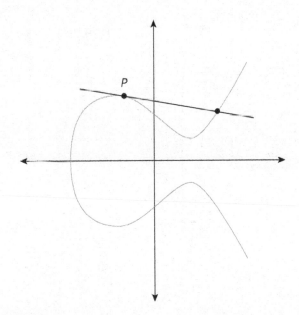

Figure 5.20 Single point start.

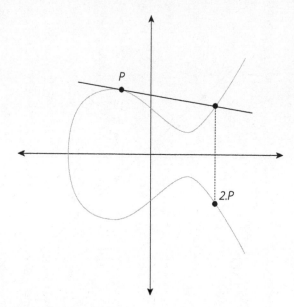

Figure 5.21 Creation of second point.

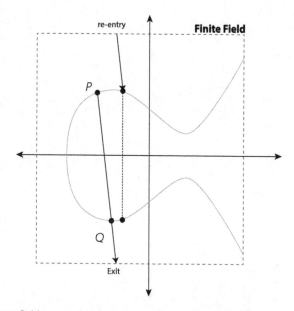

Figure 5.22 Finite field.

If the line does not coincide with the curve for a third time, or if it goes out of range before this happens, it will reach the edge of a bounding box and move to the other side and continue at the same angle (fig 5.22).

So, starting with P, we have seen that we can add to that to create 2.P, 3.P 4.P and so on. We also have methods to work out the following numbers by using regular type addition, so in the same way that

$$2+3=5$$

We can also calculate

$$2.P + 3.P = 5.P$$

With this in mind, if I asked you to work out point 66, you would be able to do it in just a few point calculations. That would work something like this:

$$P+P=2P$$

$$2P+2P=4P$$

$$4P+4P=8P$$

$$8P+8P=16P$$

$$16P+16P=32P$$

$$32P+32P=64P$$

$$64P+2P=66P$$

This makes things a lot faster. If I gave you even a very large number, you would be able to calculate it in a relatively small number of steps. Most cryptocurrencies use integers up to 2^{256}, that's $1.1579209e+77$, a 78-digit number! If I pick a number anywhere in that range, by adding up in this way, it would take up to a maximum of 510 steps to calculate any point, so long as I start knowing the number of steps – so in the example above the number of steps is 66.

If, however, I gave you a point and asked you to work out how many steps it took to reach that point, you would need to work it out by adding to P in repetition and testing the values to see if they matched. This, however, is very costly in terms of time. If we are storing the integer value using 256 bits, we have seen that there are $1.1579209e + 77$ different possible values. That's a very large number! Even with a supercomputer, you would be working it out for many millennia to come.

In private and public keys, the number of steps is used as a private key and the resultant point is used as the public key. Remembering what we have learned about public and private keys, you will know that it should be possible to derive the public key from the private key, but not the other way round. ECC is how we achieve this.

Key points about ECC

- In ECC we use an Elliptic Curve and use a starting point.
- We can then move to the next point by drawing a line between the two points and looking for the next intersection.
- It is possible to add and multiply the points together to work out later points.
- It is not possible to subtract or divide points to work backwards.
- The private key is the number of steps to get from one point to another.
- The public key is the point that we arrive at.

WALLETS AND KEYS

Wallets are, in their most basic form, just private keys. That private key is used to sign transactions so that the blockchain can determine where a transaction is coming from and validate its authenticity. A public key is derived from this and this is used to receive funds. This is a one-way process. You can always generate a public key from a private key, but it is practically impossible to generate the private key from the public key. A suitable analogy would be to consider the public key to be like your bank account number, which is used to receive funds and the private key to be like your PIN which you use to authorize transactions. People can know your account number, but you should never make your PIN public.

In Bitcoin, for example, a public key is derived from the private key and a Bitcoin address is derived from the public key. This is what you use to receive transactions. To receive funds to that address, a transaction with valid funding is created and signed using a private key and sent you your Bitcoin address. We will look at transactions in more detail later.

System	Valid characters used to represent numbers
Decimal (Base-10)	0, 1, 2, 3, 4, 5, 6, 7, 8, 9
Hexadecimal (Base-16)	0, 1, 2, 3, 4, 5, 6, 7, 8, 9, A, B, C, D, E, F
Base-58	1, 2, 3, 4, 5, 6, 7, 8, 9, A, B, C, D, E, F, G, H, J, K, L, M, N, P, Q, R, S, T, U, V, W, X, Y, Z, a, b, c, d, e, f, g, h, i, j, k, m, n, o, p, q, r, s, t, u, v, w, x, y, z
Base-64	0, 1, 2, 3, 4, 5, 6, 7, 8, 9, A, B, C, D, E, F, G, H, I, J, K, L, M, N, O, P, Q, R, S, T, U, V, W, X, Y, Z, a, b, c, d, e, f, g, h, i, j, k, l, m, n, o, p, q, r, s, t, u, v, w, x, y, z, +, /

Figure 5.23 Character representation of numbers.

BASE-58

Addresses are typically represented as base-58. If decimal is a way of representing numbers with characters 0-9 and hexadecimal is a way of representing numbers using base-16, with characters 0-F, base-58 uses further letters of the alphabet, to extend the base.

Base-58 was derived from base-64, where all letters and numbers, as well as the + and / symbols, are used to represent numbers. The only modification to this was to remove the symbols and remove letters and numbers that might easily be confused for each other. You can see from the table above that, missing from the normal alphabet and numbers are uppercase I, lowercase L, Capital O and the number zero (I, l, O and 0). This is because they would be confusing when written or printed and could cause errors.

Note: There is more than one version of base-58. The different versions order the characters in different ways, so simply specifying base-58 is not enough to define this in the same way it would be with hexadecimal.

The process of creation of the keys and their exact encoding varies, but it can loosely be considered as being represented by the figure 5.26.

Any public/private key pair is a valid wallet. With very little exception, these are held and managed by computers, but it is quite possible to create a valid wallet without using a computer and so transactions could be sent by text message, email or even a phone call.

Value	Character	Value	Character	Value	Character	Value	Character
0	1	1	2	2	3	3	4
4	5	5	6	6	7	7	8
8	9	9	A	10	B	11	C
12	D	13	E	14	F	15	G
16	H	17	J	18	K	19	L
20	M	21	N	22	P	23	Q
24	R	25	S	26	T	27	U
28	V	29	W	30	X	31	Y
32	Z	33	a	34	b	35	c
36	d	37	e	38	f	39	g
40	h	41	i	42	j	43	k
44	m	45	n	46	o	47	p
48	q	49	r	50	s	51	t
52	u	53	v	54	w	55	x
56	y	57	z				

Figure 5.24 Base-58.

Decimal value	Base-58 Conversion	Decimal value	Base-58 Conversion
1	2	76	2K
55	x	128	3D

Figure 5.25 Base-58 examples.

Sometimes you will see the wallet address as a QR code. This can make things more convenient when transacting, as one wrong character may well result in lost funds (fig 5.27).

Around the public and private keys, wallets are usually built on applications that can query the blockchain to determine the funds that you have available to you and create transactions using your private key and broadcast them to the Bitcoin network.

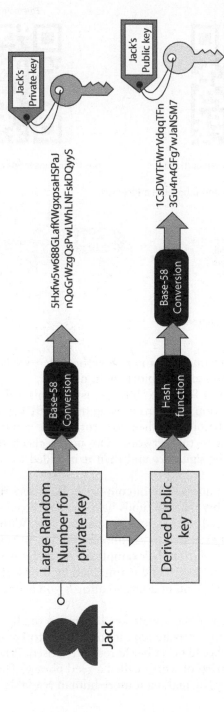

Figure 5.26 Base-58 keys.

Bitcoin address

32ZhJoZdpEG24ZSK6SHBqH91uuu4j1XJBR

Ethereum address

0x431C01e7FcA890f89742eb92357406ef968700ad

Figure 5.27 My Bitcoin and Ethereum addresses.

Figure 5.28 Signed transaction.

Let's look at an example that puts together what we have learned about encryption, signatures and the blockchain network.

Jack wants to send 1 Bitcoin to Jill. He instructs his wallet to do this and it constructs a transaction and signs it using his private key (fig 5.28). We will look more at transactions and their structure in the coming section.

This is broadcast to the network. The nodes check the validity of the transaction using the signature and then it is added to the blockchain (fig 5.29).

When Jill's wallet queries the Bitcoin network, it sees the funds allocated to her and informs her that the funds have been received (fig 5.30).

Wallets can be stored on a full node or a partial node. With cryptocurrencies, the partial nodes are referred to as simplified payment verification or SPVs. You may be able to see from the example above that a wallet does not store coins. All assets are managed and maintained by the blockchain. The wallet stores your private key and in doing so affords you access to the assets held on the blockchain.

Because the holder of the private key has access to all the funds stored on the blockchain by that private key, it should be stored as securely as possible. Private keys should never be shared or exposed. Private keys are often generated from a string of words called a seed phrase. This makes an easier way of storing a key, by making it more human readable (fig 5.31).

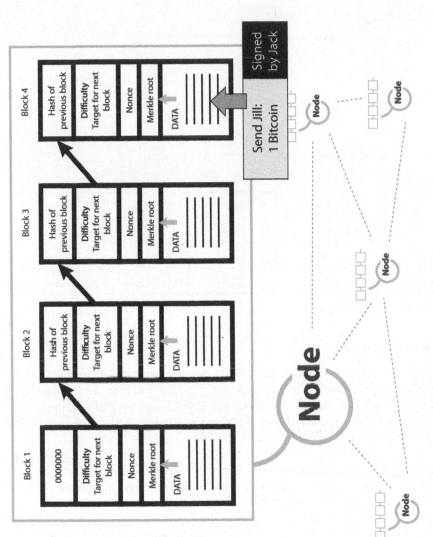

Figure 5.29 Signed transaction on the blockchain.

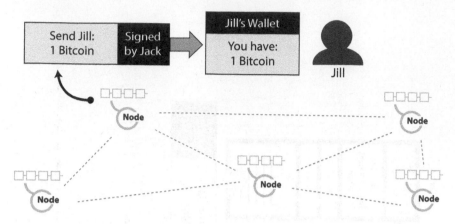

Figure 5.30 Checking your balance.

1	License	5	Pattern	9	Rail	13	Secret	17	Extend
2	Genuine	6	Girl	10	Dizzy	14	Nose	18	Elbow
3	Laptop	7	Tank	11	Soup	15	Zoo	19	Husband
4	Bamboo	8	Canal	12	Gas	16	Doctor	20	Cake

Figure 5.31 Example key phrases.

WALLET TYPES

The wallet type we describe above is what is commonly referred to as a *hot wallet*. That is to say that it has access to the internet. There are clear advantages of this, such as ease of access. If you want to send a transaction, you just need to ask the wallet to transfer the funds.

Another type of wallet is a *cold wallet*. As you might have guessed, this is an offline wallet. Typically, these wallets are some form of a hardware wallet that stores the private key inside. It never leaves the cold wallet. This is connected to a computer to provide an interface to interact with the wallet.

When the cold wallet owner wants to initiate a transaction, the request is sent to the device, the device asks for user authentication, then if successful, it will create and sign the transaction. Then it is sent to the computer for broadcasting to the network (fig 5.32).

The private key never leaves the device and is stored using encryption that means even if the wallet is stolen, the thief cannot access the funds on it. You may also restore the wallet so long as you have kept the seed phrase that was used to create the private key.

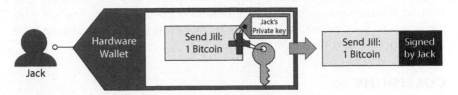

Figure 5.32 Hardware wallet.

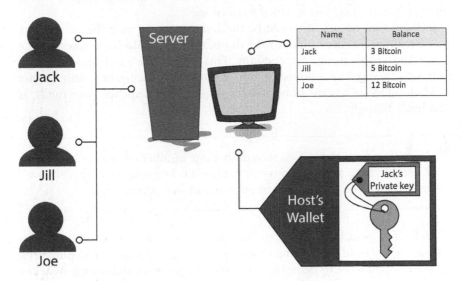

Figure 5.33 Hosted wallet.

HOSTED WALLETS

Often you will see services that offer quick exchanges between cryptocurrencies and fiat or other cryptocurrencies, typically through an app or web interface. These are often referred to as hosted wallets or non-custodial wallets. If you have a hosted wallet, the chances are great that you do not have a cryptocurrency wallet of your own. Typically, the wallet held by the hosted service contains many people's cryptocurrency assets in one wallet of their own and then allows you to control the assets that you own.

This has some benefits, such as quick and simple access to a single central service. It also has some drawbacks. For example, by centralizing the service and not holding your keys, your assets are again outside of your control. If the service stops trading, you may be unable to access your cryptocurrencies.

Though you can give other people your public key so that they can transfer funds to you, private keys should never be given out. Anyone who has access to your private key can sign transactions from you and spend the funds allocated to it on the blockchain.

COLLISIONS

Given that your private key is a randomly generated number, or more specifically a number generated from a randomly selected set of keywords, this number may be generated more than once. When a key is generated that is already in existence, this is called a collision.

If a collision occurs, it would be the same outcome as if the private key had been shared. The holder of the duplicate key would have access to the funds and be able to sign transactions. This sounds like a terrible outcome if you have invested an amount of money into a cryptocurrency, only to lose it when someone has the same address generated and spends your funds. Is this likely though?

Note: Fun fact: there is an incredibly large number of private keys in Bitcoin. There are 10^{77} possible addresses. For reference, there are estimated to be 10^{80} atoms in existence in our universe.

Well, it is possible, but given the massive amount of possible Bitcoin addresses, it would take a long time to generate a key that had already been created. If you were to dedicate your processing power to hashing new key combinations to find and steal someone's funds, you would earn significantly less than you would by dedicating your computer's processing time to creating new blocks. So, while it is possible, it is highly improbably and there is little incentive for such an attack.

Key points about wallets

- Wallets are a public and private key pair where the public key is derived from the private key.
- The private key is used to sign transactions.
- The public key or derivatives of the public key are used to track and receive funds.
- They are typically encoded into base-58.

- There are different types of wallets,
  - Hot wallets are typically connected to the internet and allow for quick transmission
  - Cold wallets store the private key in a secure device, which it never leaves for added security
  - Hosted wallets are not wallets at all they are an account with an organization who holds your assets.
- Collisions are possible but improbable.

Chapter 6

Coins and transactions

In this section, we will look at the structure of transactions and how they are processed by the cryptocurrency blockchain. Again, there are many cryptocurrencies and some of them vary these structures and processes, so we will use Bitcoin as the example on which others were derived.

What we already know about transactions:

- They are stored on the blockchain as part of the data payload.
- They are hashed using Merkle trees to prevent subsequent changes.
- They are signed using private keys and sent to an address derived from this private key.
- They are often derived from a series of words.

Note: A block can contain many transactions. Bitcoin for example can process around 2000 transactions per block.

When people talk about cryptocurrencies, you will often hear them refer to coins. As we have discussed already, any allocation of assets exists only on the blockchain and not on the wallets. In some cases, the balance is held as values. This is referred to as the *account model*. In other cases, balances are only calculated based on transactions that exist and anything that is unspent from these transactions. Transactions are often abbreviated to TX and unspent transaction outputs are UTXOs for short. This is known as the *UTXO model*.

Regardless of whether balances are held, or whether we have only UTXOs, the term coin is a familiar idea from traditional finance, applied in a way that is arguably inaccurate but helps us understand and relate to the new system. We will look at both of these methods, but before we do, we need to talk about fungible and non-fungible assets.

DOI: 10.1201/9781003187165-6

FUNGIBLE AND NON-FUNGIBLE ASSETS

It doesn't take long in the blockchain world to come across the terms fungible and non-fungible. Fungibility can be considered to be interchangeability. Some assets like, for example, gold bars, are gold bars. If you own a gold bar, assuming they are standardized in weight, it is interchangeable for any other gold bar. Other things, like the Mona Lisa, are not. You could not simply replace it with another copy and so it is non-fungible.

Examples of fungible assets: red house bricks, gold bars and stocks.

Examples of non-fungible assets: artwork, snowflakes, houses and estates and precious gems.

What category a dollar would fall into is arguable, but most people consider them to be fungible, as people really don't care which dollar they have and nor can they generally tell. They are serialized, however, so it could be argued that they can be distinguished from each other and so one is not completely interchangeable with another. Largely the same is said of most cryptocurrencies and though this is true for the most part, the whole truth shows that it is not as black and white as perhaps it first appears.

One key difference between fungible and non-fungible assets is the ability to track an asset's history. For a non-fungible asset such as a painting, it is possible, assuming accurate records are kept, for the exact ownership of that asset to be tracked over time. Assuming the same accurate record taking, it is likely to be impossible to track the exact history of that asset. For example, if I paid you $1 and you added it to your bank account and went out on a shopping spree, spending all the funds from your account, you would not be able to tell what it was you spent that exact dollar on, because it is not possible to tell it from the other dollars.

Fungibility can become an issue when you want to track assets, for example if you wanted to return stolen funds to their owners. Asset tracking has been used to locate and monitor illegitimately obtained cryptocurrency which has occasionally led to its return. It is also relevant concerning auditing and transparency, due to the clarity of which assets have gone where. Blockchains can be used to transact with fungible and non-fungible assets and the approach to asset management needs to be considerate of fungibility issues.

UTXO MODEL

In the UTXO model, there are no account balances stored per se; instead, transactions have inputs and outputs. Any assets that you own are the result of having received them but not having spent them. With this model, it is possible to determine the exact coin and its history as it has been passed around from account to account and so it has a lower level of fungibility than with the account model, which we will discuss later.

Figure 6.1 A transaction.

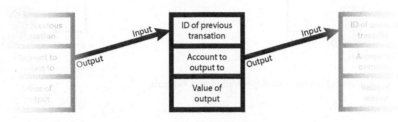

Figure 6.2 A transaction structure.

As no balance is stored, to determine your balance, you must look through the chain of transactions and determine what has been sent to you and not-yet spent, that it is a UTXO.

The input and output must be equal. This includes the fee paid to the miner that adds the transaction to the blockchain. This means that

$$input = output + transaction\,fee.$$

In the image above, 1 coin goes in and 0.95 coins go out. Because the input must equal the output + transaction fee, we can see that the fee paid for this transaction is 0.05 coins. The fee is never stated explicitly but can be easily worked out when looking at a transaction. As you can tell, cryptocurrencies use divisions of the coin. In Bitcoin, for example, the smallest unit is a Satoshi, which is equal to 100,000,000th of a Bitcoin.

Again, we will start with a simple model and build up our understanding. Currently, our transaction structure looks like this (fig 6.2).

Note that the inputs to one transaction are the outputs from previous ones. You can see that the input value is also not explicitly stated. This is because all available funds or UTXO from the output of the previous transaction will be used as the input.

You might be asking yourself what happens when you only want to use a fraction of the available funds and the answer is provided by using multiple outputs. In the above example, we saw a transaction with one input and

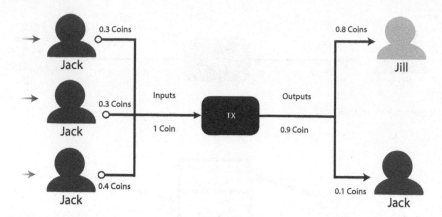

Figure 6.3 A transaction with multiple inputs and outputs.

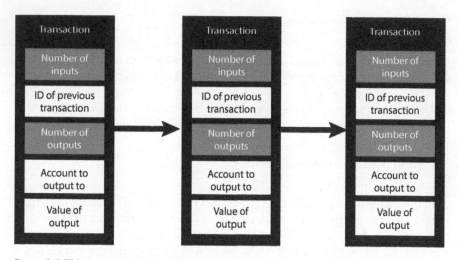

Figure 6.4 TX structure with inputs and outputs.

one output. It is common, however, for transactions to have multiple inputs and outputs. It is using this that we handle partial spending. Let's look at another example (fig 6.3).

To accommodate these multiple inputs and outputs we are going to have to add some pieces of information to our transactions structure. We are going to need to tell it how many inputs and outputs to expect and provide information about those inputs and outputs. For this reason, we are going to add "input counter" and "output counter". We will then repeat the input and output section the same number of time as we have inputs and outputs.

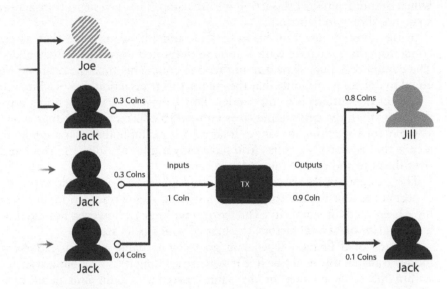

Figure 6.5 Inputs from previous TX.

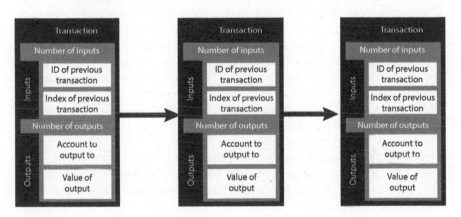

Figure 6.6 TX with indices.

For simplicity, these transaction blocks show a single transaction output linked to a single transaction input. The white input and output sections are repeated once for each input and output. Returning to our previous example, consider if our input was the result of multiple outputs (fig 6.5).

We can see that the input coming from the top left comes from a transaction that had two outputs, one to Joe and one to Jack. This means for us to use the UTXO in our new transaction, to define where the funds come from, we don't just need to state the previous transaction ID, we also need to tell it which output from the transaction we are using. That gives us a transaction structure shown in figure 6.6.

In the above transaction between Jack and Jill, we can see that assets come from three separate wallets and are outputted to two separate wallets. The combined inputs again amount to one coin. This time the outputs are equal to 0.9 coins, meaning that the fee for this transaction was 0.1 Bitcoin.

One of the outputs is to the sender. This is how we handle sending anything less than the entire input. It is comparable to receiving change when you pay for something in a shop. Imagine for example that you are buying a cake that is worth six coins. You have only a note of value 10. You hand over the note and receive four coins in return.

The fees paid in the example above are higher than one would typically expect at the time of publishing, for conducting such a transaction, but they have been used for simplicity. The fee you will pay is, however, not fixed. It is dependent on several factors, the first of which is its size.

In traditional finance, when you go to your bank and you request a money transfer, this might be free if you are sending it using a bank transfer within the same country in the same currency. Credit and debit card transactions or transnational transfers, however, may be charged using flat rate fees, percentages of the total value transferred or combinations of both. Cryptocurrencies do not set fees based on how large the transfer value is, the fee is instead dependent on the size that the transaction takes up in bytes.

Imagine that you are adding transactions into the blockchain. You have a set maximum block size. You have a list of many transactions to choose from that you could add to your block. You want to fit as many transactions into the maximum block size as possible to get the greatest total fee as possible. You will have two considerations; how many bytes is the transaction taking up and how much fee is it giving me per byte. You can see then that transactions in a blockchain are paid in Satoshi per byte.

In figure 6.7, given the available transactions and constraints, the miner would most likely construct the right block for adding to the blockchain, because they receive a higher level of fee for this block compared to the other, in Satoshi per byte.

You can select the fee that you allocate. The higher the fee, the quicker the item is likely to be processed as it will be more likely to be selected for inclusion in the block by the system that processes it. This is typically done by the wallet and some wallets allow for the selection of larger fees with quicker processing time and lower fees with slower processing times.

If you have funds received from previous transactions, you might have 1 coin, but it could be the output of several transactions. This can mean if you were to move it to another wallet, it might have more inputs and 1 output. In the diagram you will see the holder of the same amount of coins, transferring the same amount to the same place; the only difference is that one of them has UTXOs from one source and the other from multiple sources.

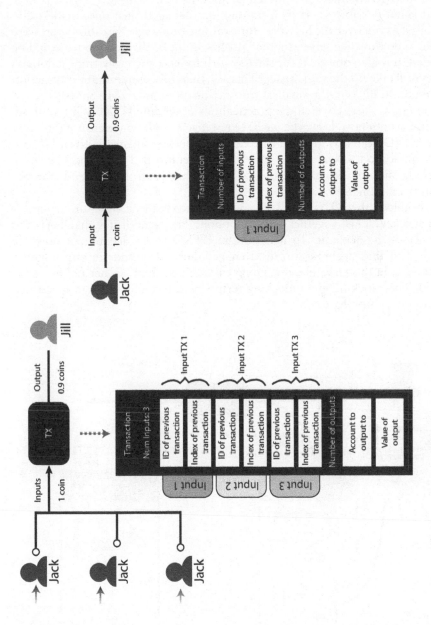

Figure 6.7 Example transaction and sizes.

The second is larger to store and therefore typically costs more to transact. Though this would appear the same in your wallet, the left one would likely cost more to conduct the transaction than the right would.

It is not possible to create a transaction that sends just one smallest division of a coin over the network, for example one single Satoshi. If you were able to do this then, given that a Satoshi cannot be divided, no fee could be added. It is also not great for the network to have such tiny transactions as they still take up the same space. There is, therefore, a minimum transaction amount. In Bitcoin, the smallest transaction amount is 5340 Satoshis.

So far, we have covered the practicalities of sending UTXOs in a transaction. Up until now, however, we have not discussed how we ensure that only the UTXO holder is allowed to create transactions against a given UTXO. The ability to transact with a give UTXO is controlled by scripts. They are locking and unlocking signatures and keys that control whether a transaction is valid (fig 6.8).

To unlock the UTXO for Jack to spend, he creates a signature using his private key. This, together with his public key, establishes that he is the owner of the account. To allocate the UTXO to an account, it must be locked to that account so only that account can authorize any ongoing transfers. In this example, it is going to Jane's account, so her public key is used. These locking and unlocking scripts need to be included in our transaction structure (fig 6.9)

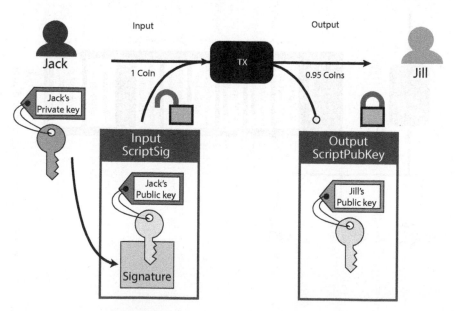

Figure 6.8 Locking and unlocking scripts.

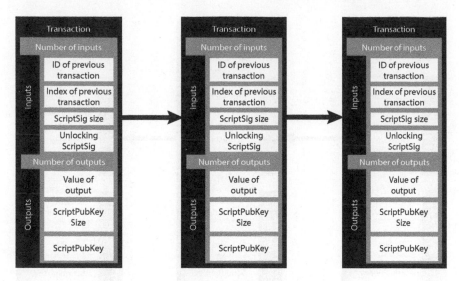

Figure 6.9 TX with locking and unlocking scripts.

We have added in a couple of things here, besides the SriptSig and ScriptPubKey: we have also added a size element, to tell anything processing the transaction how long to expect the script to be.

The use of scripts not only checks that the transaction creator is allowed to conduct the transaction but also allows for the creation of transactions that need to be signed by multiple separate keys. This is useful, for example, if you have a business partner and you must both agree before spending funds. This is comparable to a bankcheque that requires two signatures from both account holders. It is possible to create more complex unlocking scripts, which require many more people to authorize the unlocking, or perhaps are unlocked through a password instead.

We have just a couple of things left to add to our transaction structure. Let's add them in now:

If you look at the following diagram you will see that I have also added an element for "version" that tells us what version of the transaction block to expect. This will help us if there are updates to the transaction block format. We discussed forks earlier on and the effects that they can have on a network of blockchain nodes. By providing a version number, we can build in levels of backward compatibility with updates, to reduce the impact of the update.

Lastly, we have added in lock time, which allows us to specify a minimum block height or time in which the transaction can be included, creating a timed execution of the transaction.

For simplicity, we have drawn the transactions in figure 6.10 as single input and single output transactions, but the blockchain for cryptocurrencies

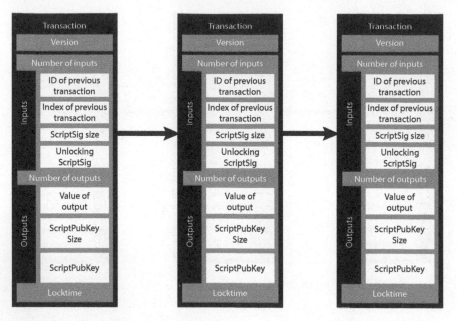

Figure 6.10 Lastly a TX with lock time.

is essentially a long branching chain of transactions, including their inputs and outputs (fig 6.11).

It is possible to determine from this the UTXOs allocated to any given account. Given that the blockchain is public and readable by anyone with a suitable computer and software, it is possible to track the entire history of a UTXO. This makes auditing much simpler and more transparent.

The first transaction in the block is often the block reward. This is a reward fee paid to miners, for the effort and energy they put in mining on the system. It is, therefore, new currency and has no input.

Note: Some people will pay a premium for new UTXOs as they have no history. In the real world, when you receive an asset, be it a television you purchased or a payment of cash you received by bank transfer, the history of that asset can become relevant, for example, if it turned out to be stolen at some point before you acquired it. "Clean" coins are considered as desirable, therefore, by some, for their lack of history.

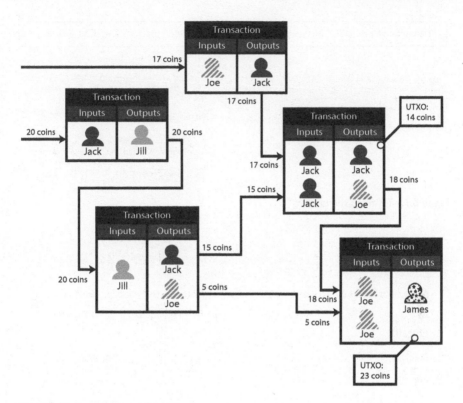

Figure 6.11 A web of transactions.

Because the Bitcoin blockchain is public, we can look at the actual transactions in the block. Let's look at a real transaction (fig 6.12).

We can see that the transaction has one input and two outputs. It is possible that the output was to a single wallet and the other was a return of the change. We do not necessarily know who conducted the transaction, however, with the increase of Know Your Customer (KYC) regulation, the anonymity of transactions has been reduced.

Let's have a look at another from the blockchain (fig 6.13).

We can see that this block has one confirmation. This means that it was in the most current block at the time of writing. You can see that one of the outputs matches the inputs, which indicates a return of change. The fee is listed in Satoshi per byte.

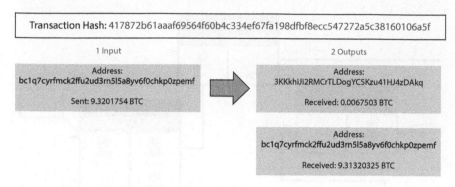

Figure 6.12 TX from the block.

TX Hash: 79e8154af30fe82bc1e8a139d2dde4e1ee75cdfdc65f143ad3cfd9f4e4f6ad1e

bc1qrusqjsg3dag3qk...   0.52391408 BTC   ➡   bc1qf2x5nay7y6rh0w...   0.02949600 BTC

                                              bc1qrusqjsg3dag3qk...   0.49415864 BTC

Details

Date	29th of July, 2021
Time	10:50 am
Age	6 minutes ago
Fees	116 Sat
Included in block	693198
Confirmations	1

Figure 6.13 TX with one confirmation.

ACCOUNT MODEL

The account model is probably easier to consider, as it will likely be closer to what you will be familiar with. It essentially stores and tracks values in much the same way as a bank account does. A transaction that adds one coin to your account leads to an updating on the value held against you in the blockchain.

This diagram based on the method described in the Ethereum white paper (Ethereum.org 2021) outlines how this works (fig 6.16).

You can see that, rather than using UTXOs, a transaction initiates a value transfer from one account (fpz68b) to another (5dp9x0). It is the value that updated rather than the transfer of an asset between accounts. This leads to higher asset fungibility. In the same way as the example we used previously of shopping and not-knowing which dollar was spent on which item, if you

TX Hash: 79e8154af30fe82bc1e8a139d2dde4e1ee75cdfdc65f143ad3cfd9f4e4f6ad1e

Input details

Index	0
Address	bc1qrusqjsg3dag3qkgcn3ysnw7xwxy76eqm5sh3rw
Amount	0.52391408 BTC

Figure 6.14 TX inputs.

Output details (2 Outputs)

Index	0
Address	bc1qf2x5nay7y6rh0w8yw7fa2et7xxg0eqxt2u5ext
Amount	0.02949600 BTC

Index	1
Address	bc1qrusqjsg3dag3qkgcn3ysnw7xwxy76eqm5sh3rw
Amount	0.49415864 BTC

Figure 6.15 TX outputs.

receive a coin and send a coin from your balance, it is not possible to track the history of that particular coin.

Let's have a look at some actual transactions from the Ethereum network (fig 6.17).

Many of the elements are the same or similar to those we have seen before while exploring blocks that use the UTXO model. You may have noticed that the output is labelled "contract". We will discuss this in the section on smart contracts.

Key points about transactions

- Transactions and how they are managed affect the fungibility of the assets being transferred.
- Selection of transactions for inclusion in a block is typically done based on fee paid/size in bytes.
- Access to the funds in a transaction would normally be managed by locking and unlocking scripts.

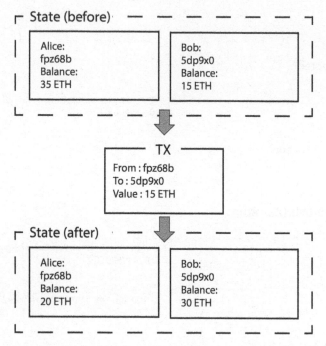

Figure 6.16 Account model based on method outlined in Ethereum white paper (Ethereum. org 2021).

- There are two distinct mechanisms for managing transactions: the UTXO model and the account/balance model.
  - UTXO:
    - Transaction blocks contain a list of inputs and their index from the incoming transaction.
  - Account/balance model
    - Transactions update balances for given accounts.

MIXERS

Also known as tumblers, coin mixers aim to obscure the history of assets. They do this by using a series of transactions to a shared account. Several accounts add funds to a shared location. From there several transactions withdraw funds from the account. For additional security, this could be to a separate wallet.

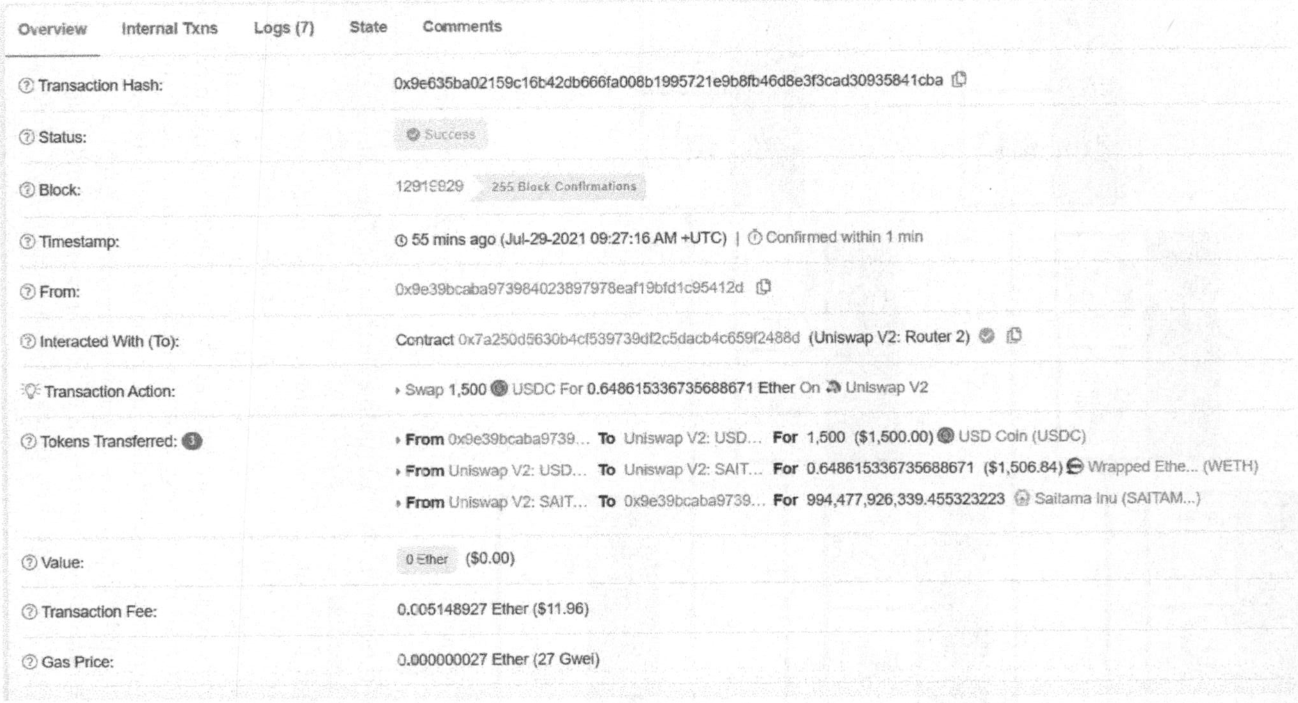

Overview	Internal Txns	Logs (7)	State	Comments

⑦ Transaction Hash: 0x9e635ba02159c16t42db666fa008b1995721e9b8fb46d8e3f3cad30935841cba

⑦ Status: ● Success

⑧ Block: 12916929   255 Block Confirmations

⑦ Timestamp: ⏱ 55 mins ago (Jul-29-2021 09:27:16 AM +UTC) | ⏱ Confirmed within 1 min

⑦ From: 0x9e39bcaba973984023897978eaf19bfd1c95412d

⑦ Interacted With (To): Contract 0x7a250d5630b4cf539739df2c5dacb4c659f2488d   (Uniswap V2: Router 2)

⑦ Transaction Action: ▸ Swap 1,500 ● USDC For 0.648615336735688671 Ether On ⚫ Uniswap V2

⑦ Tokens Transferred: ⑤
▸ **From** 0x9e39bcaba9739... **To** Uniswap V2: USD... **For** 1,500 ($1,500.00) ● USD Coin (USDC)
▸ **From** Uniswap V2: USD... **To** Uniswap V2: SAIT... **For** 0.648615336735688671 ($1,506.84) ⊖ Wrapped Ethe... (WETH)
▸ **From** Uniswap V2: SAIT... **To** 0x9e39bcaba9739... **For** 994,477,926,339.455323223 ⊕ Saitama Inu (SAITAM...)

⑦ Value: 0 Ether   ($0.00)

⑦ Transaction Fee: 0.05148927 Ether ($11.96)

⑦ Gas Price: 0.000000027 Ether (27 Gwei)

Figure 6.17 Transaction from the Ethereum network (Etherscan 2021).

Excerpt from Etherscan.io available at https://etherscan.io/tx/0x3dcf7d9a9c2cad419965ccc9967c881652de2bd7604b8fb8943fefa3ef3433ab

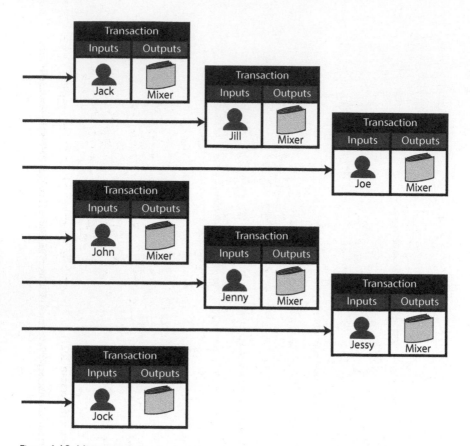

Figure 6.18 Mixer inputs.

Imagine seven people want to tumble their coins. They all add their coins to the same account.

Their funds are sent, over some time, to a secondary wallet from the shared account. Often this is in smaller transactions, and the process may be repeated over randomized periods so that one cannot simply match quantities and times together by looking at the data held on the blockchain. Generally, you will receive several coins back from the same account, but no one withdrawer will receive the same coins that they submitted, breaking the link between the depositor and the withdrawer (fig 6.19).

Each of the transactions to the wallet is split among some of the receivers until they have received all their funds back, minus the fees. Here one transaction is shown.

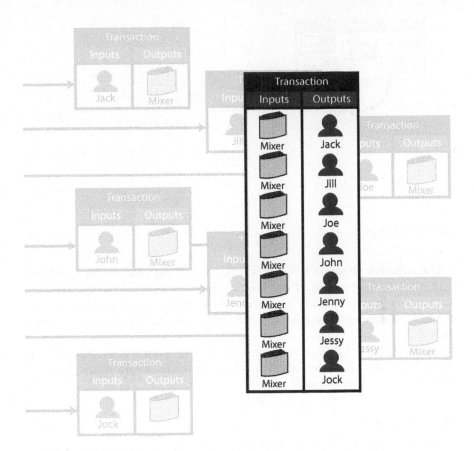

Figure 6.19 Mixer outputs.

MEMPOOL

When a transaction is broadcast, the nodes that receive it validate it and add it to the mempool. This is a store of all the transactions waiting to be added to the blockchain. Nodes store and share their mempool entries. Transactions are then selected from the mempool to go into the block.

Each block will have a maximum size defined by the protocol. For Bitcoin this is 1 mb. When there is a lot of data waiting in the mempool, the wait time for that data to enter the chain increases. This can have implications for users. In Bitcoin, for example, a large number of transactions in the mempool means more time waiting to be processed and that the cost of the transaction is likely to go up as you have to pay more to get picked from all the other transactions waiting in the mempool.

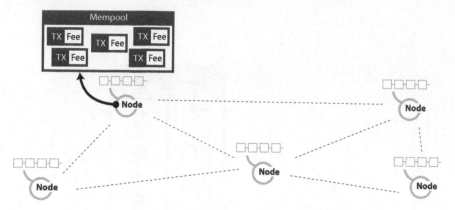

Figure 6.20 Mempool.

The different shades on the graph (fig 6.21) indicate the fee level per byte, with the lower fees at the bottom and the higher fees near the top. You can see that the lower fees are picked with a lower preference. The mempool drops as transactions are added to the block and removed from the mempool.

In the event of accidental forks, when blocks are orphaned, the transactions that were present in them are effectively returned to the mempool, for processing in subsequent blocks.

REFERENCES

Ethereum.org (2021) *Ethereum White Paper.* Available at https://ethereum.org/en/whitepaper/ [Accessed 29 July 2021].

Etherscan (2021) *Transaction Details.* Available at https://etherscan.io/tx/0x3dc f7d9a9c2cad419965ccc9967c881652de2bd7604b8fb8943fefa3ef3433ab [Accessed 29 July 2021].

The Mempool Open Source Project (2021) *Mempool by vBytes.* Available at https://mempool.space/graphs [Accessed 28 July 2021].

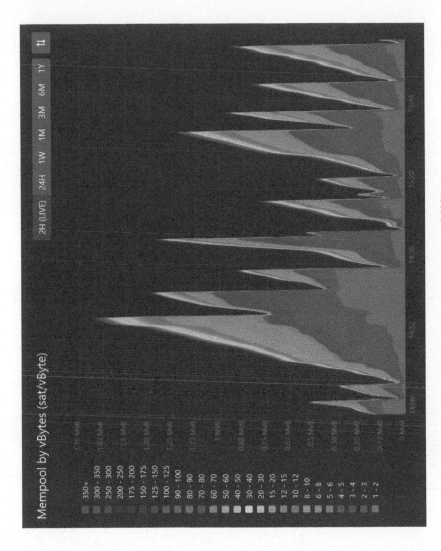

Figure 6.21 Mempool chart (The Mempool Open Source Project 2021).

Chapter 7

Mining

We have touched on various aspects of mining out of necessity to explain the concepts in the previous chapters. Let's summarize what we already know:

- Miners are nodes that can write to the chain.
- They can select the transactions that they add into a new block.
- They receive transaction fees for the transactions in the blocks they add to the blockchain.
- They can receive a block reward for adding blocks to the blockchain.
- Miners compete with each other to guess a valid hash which allows them to append their block to the chain.
- Miners provide security to the network through Proof of Work.
- They guess nonces to meet a changeable difficulty target that is varied to keep block creation times separated.

This activity got its name because of the notion of a node receiving a reward for its work and the comparison to mining for gold, diamonds or other precious items. The work that you put in is rewarded by the discovery of new resources.

We have already been introduced to the concept of Proof of Work and how it secures the network by requiring work. Proof of Work is a *consensus mechanism* that requires computational work to be able to contribute to a blockchain. Though it is probably the most commonly used and best understood, it is not the only consensus mechanism, so we will look at Proof of Work and the other commonly used consensus mechanisms too.

CONSENSUS MECHANISMS

Consensus mechanisms like Proof of Work are a method of making sure that all nodes on the network agree and that they all act fairly. They include mechanisms that allow the network to agree on what gets added by whom and ensure that no one person or group of people can take over the network and change the contents of the blockchain.

DOI: 10.1201/9781003187165-7

PROOF OF WORK (PoW)

The concept of Proof of Work can be defined as keeping miners investing energy in finding valid nonces that allow the block hash to meet the target. There are several features of the Proof of Work model that are essential to its operation.

1. The work should be difficult. If the work is not difficult then a small amount of work is all that is needed to retrospectively change the contents of the blockchain. This is achieved by making the miners create many guesses and hashes to find a valid nonce. This costs the miner running costs in electricity and potentially other costs such as hardware, facilities, etc.
2. The work should be easy to check. In order to make it efficient to validate the contents of the blockchain, checking the solution to the work done needs to be easy to do.
3. The amount of work required needs to be variable. As new miners can join or leave the network, the overall work done by the collective systems can vary greatly. You may hear of the hash power of the network being referred to.

   The hash power of the network affects the amount of time it takes to mine new blocks. To maintain block size the difficulty of the mining task needs to be varied. This variability is achieved by modifying the

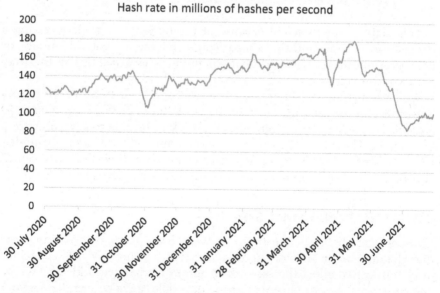

Figure 7.1 The Bitcoin hash rate.

difficulty target based on the average production time of the blocks. For Bitcoin, if the average block time increases above 10 minutes, the difficulty is reduced. If it decreases to below 10 minutes, the difficulty increases.

4. The network should invest in the chain with the most work. This means that nodes on the system will switch in preference to the longest chain as it has had the most work invested in it. Assuming that most miners on the system are honest, by investing in the longest chain we are securing the network.

Miners compete against each other, so as hardware improves, they must update and miners with older software cannot stay profitable. As each hash is a guess at finding the next valid nonce, each guess is like a lottery ticket that can win you cryptocurrency. The more hashes you produce in the shortest time, the more tickets to that lottery you have. Mining units have two primary considerations, therefore:

1. Generate as many hashes as possible in the shortest possible time.
2. Consume as little energy as possible in doing this.

Mining power is typically measured in hashes per second. This is done as in other areas of computing, using the prefixes Kilo, Mega, Giga and Tera to denote multiples of thousands, millions, billions and trillions, respectively.

Here you can see the Antminer S19, producing 110 TeraHashes per second (TH/s).

You might also see this measured in Solutions per second (Sol/s).

Make and model:	Antminer S19 Pro
Crypto Algorithm:	SHA-256
Hashrate, TH/s	110 ± 3%
Power, Watts, at 25°C	3250 ± 5%
Power efficiency, J/TH, at 25°C	29.5 ± 5%
Networking connection mode	RJ45 Ethernet 10/100M
Miner Size (Length*Width*Height, with package), mm	570*316*430
Gross weight, kg	15.2

Figure 7.2 Antminer S19 Pro specifications.

Source: Bitmain 2021.

Make and model:	Antminer Z15 Pro
Crypto Algorithm:	EquiHash/Zcash
Hashrate, KSol/s	420
Power, Watts, at 25°C	1510
Power efficiency, J/KSol, at 25°C	3.60
Networking connection mode	RJ45 Ethernet 10/100M
Miner Size (Length*Width*Height, with package), mm	245*132.5*290
Gross weight, kg	5.90

Figure 7.3 Antminer Z15 specifications.

Source: Bitmain 2021b

As we saw a moment ago, key considerations for a mining unit are electricity consumption and hash rate. A miner with a given mining rig will consume a relatively set amount of electricity and produce a relatively set number of hashes. The profitability level is dependent not only on the number of hashes they can produce and the amount of electricity they consume. They must also consider:

- The overall hash power of the network as they are competing against the other units to find the next block.
- The value of the coin that they are selling.
- The cost of the electricity that they are consuming.

PROOF OF STAKE (PoS)

This is a more recent alternative consensus mechanism to Proof of Work. It works similarly with a few key differences. It revolves around the concept of staking.

Staking refers to the holding of cryptocurrencies in a wallet, without spending them. It comes from the concept of having a stake in something; meaning that you are invested in it. Cryptocurrencies cost money and those that *hold* them, colloquially known as HODLing them, have a stake in the success of the cryptocurrency. The concept behind this is that the majority of the people holding the coin will be invested in its transparent and honest operation and so will be honest actors.

Note: HODLing is sometimes referred to as 'Hold on for Dear Life', but it originally came from a misspelling of the word 'hold' which became a meme and stuck.

In the same way that miners receive block rewards for mining blocks with the Proof of Work system, the miners in the Proof of Stake system also receive a reward based on the number of coins that they are staking.

With Proof of Stake, however, you no longer need to invest in the network through demonstrating work done through hashing. This reduces the energy consumption of the mining nodes on the network. Instead of being the next node to mine a block because you were the first to find a suitable nonce, the next block is mined by the node selected, and the chances of being that node are typically determined by the number of coins that you have staked.

The implications of consensus mechanism extend beyond the consumption of electricity and include:

- Changes in mining hardware away from systems especially developed to efficiently produce large numbers of hashes, known as ASIC units.
- Changes to behaviour. A good example of this would be that in PoW miners typically sell rewards from mined blocks to cover the large cost in electricity that mining creates. With PoS, miners will have lower running costs and be more likely to hold profits made as the profits can also be staked. These behaviour changes can have further consequences on the value of the cryptocurrency and *miner capitulation*, which we will discuss shortly.

Proof of Stake is not as common as Proof of Work currently, though there are some instances of this both in existence and in preparation. Ethereum is the second-largest cryptocurrency and its version 2.0 network will use Proof of Stake.

DELEGATED PROOF OF STAKE (DPoS)

Delegated Proof of Stake or DPoS is a modified version of Proof of Stake. In it, we add to the PoS system, a method of using stakes to determine votes. Stakers are given a say in the managing of the system. You can lend your voting power to a delegate who helps to manage to project and guide it in your desired direction.

OTHER CONSENSUS MECHANISMS

Proof of Work and Proof of Stake make up the vast majority of consensus mechanisms in blockchain, they are however not the only game in town and as time goes by, we may see others emerge and climb in popularity. One such consensus mechanism is Proof of Elapsed time.

PROOF OF ELAPSED TIME (PoET)

PoET is a mechanism which seeks to reduce the requirement for energy consumption that PoW creates. It does this in a similar manner to PoS, though rather than relying on stake quantities to determine who mines the next block, nodes receive a randomized timer. The next block is mined by the node whose timer expires first.

Because nodes do not need to produce large numbers of hashes to establish their work, it consumes much less processing power and energy. By the same token, it offers less security and therefore is less likely to be used in cryptocurrency applications. It can, however, be useful in systems in which a higher level of trust is present, such as supply chain management.

PRACTICAL BYZANTINE FAULT TOLERANCE (PBFT)

In this system one node is leader, and the others are backups. The leadership can be and usually is rotated, depending on the implementation. The nodes communicate with each other to check the actions of each other and the state is determined through majority consensus.

PROOF OF AUTHORITY AND PROOF OF REPUTATION (PoA AND PoR/PoRE)

Proof of Authority (PoA) and Proof of Reputation (PoR/PoRe) are consensus mechanisms where nodes are allowed to add to contribute blocks to the chain if they are authorized to do so and selected on their authority or reputation respectively. Typically used in inter-organizational blockchains, the concept behind this consensus mechanism is that organizations would not wish to risk their reputation by falsifying content on the blockchain. Not all companies, however, will act honestly, even large companies have been caught illegally manipulating data, such as Volkswagen faking emissions data. It is better suited to applications where there is a greater degree of trust between nodes than there are in cryptocurrencies.

MIXED METHODS

There are of course more complex arrangements possible. The cryptocurrency Zilliqa uses Practical Byzantine Fault Tolerance (PBFT) combined with PoW used to determine sharding – which is a process of subdividing the nodes into smaller groups for processing of transactions in parallel.

Regardless of the consensus mechanism, whether it is Proof of Work or Proof of Stake, or something else, the miners are typically in mining to make money. They will earn rewards and fees in the cryptocurrency and sell all or a portion of these to cover their running costs.

Key points about consensus mechanisms

- Consensus mechanisms allow the nodes on a network to agree on who is allowed to create the next block.
- They are a method of making sure that all nodes on the network agree and that they all act fairly.
- They should be easy to verify by other nodes on the network.
- They need to allow for adjustments in block time.
- In Proof of Work (PoW) nodes take guesses at nonces to find a valid nonce to make the hash meet the hash target.
- In Proof of Stake (PoS) nodes 'stake' tokens, their stake gives them a chance of being the next to create a block.
- In Proof of Elapsed Time (PoET) nodes are given timers and the next node to create a block is the node whose timer goes off first.

MINER CAPITULATION

Though we are not focusing on the financial aspects of blockchain technologies, we do need to understand something about them to understand why they happen and what the results of this are.

Typically, miner capitation takes place as a result of two things: the price of the coin dropping or competition on the network increases. The former has much more impact on the system than the latter and is therefore typically what people refer to when they talk about miner capitulation.

MINER CAPITULATION BY PRICE DROP

When the price of a cryptocurrency drops, the amount that they receive in block rewards per block remains the same, so their income drops. Depending on the price that they are paying to run the miners, this may cause them to become unprofitable. They could be spending more money on electricity and maintenance costs than they are making in selling the cryptocurrency. When this happens, many miners will switch their machines off and give up or *capitulate*.

Figure 7.4 Bitcoin price.

Source: Charting platform used for this analysis is provided by TradingView.

When this happens the hash rate of the network will drop which will cause the block time to increase and therefore the transaction time will go up. Typically, this will, as we have discussed earlier, result in a difficulty change, to bring the block time back into line with expectations.

Let's look at an example. Here you see the price chart from February–June 2020.

You can see a significant price drop from 7–12 March. Over these five days, it dropped over 50 per cent, more than 40 per cent of that in one day, on the 12th of March. This was widely reported to be as a result of the global pandemic COVID-19, and similar effects were seen in other markets. Still, we are not here to consider the financial aspects, we are interested in how the system responded to this change.

As we have discussed, the price drop leads to a miner capitulation event. Miners have switched their machines off because it is costing them more to mine than they are making in Bitcoin. This resulted in the hash rate dropping. This can be seen in figure 7.5, showing the Bitcoin hash rate.

This causes the block time to increase as there is less hash power dedicated to guessing at hashes on the network. You can see in figure 7.6, the increase above the target of 10 minutes, in the same period.

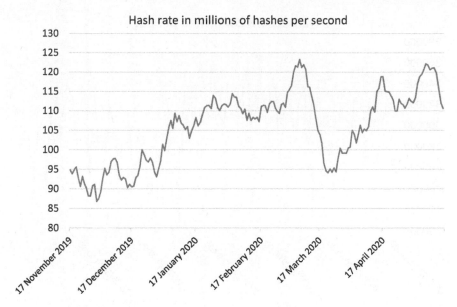

Figure 7.5 Bitcoin hash rate.

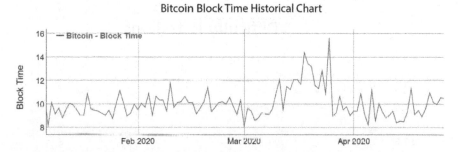

Figure 7.6 Block time.

Source: Chart reproduced with kind permission from https://bitinfocharts.com.

This means that fewer transactions can be processed at that time. Figure 7.7 shows the effect on the processing of transactions for that period.

After a number of blocks, a difficulty adjustment will take place and the mining of blocks becomes easier. The chart below shows the difficulty for that period.

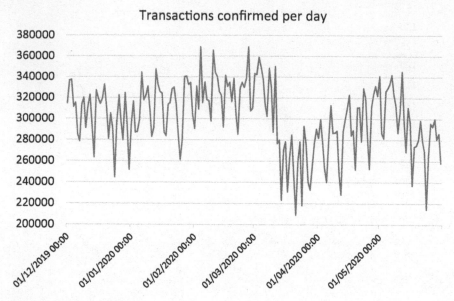

Figure 7.7 TX per second.

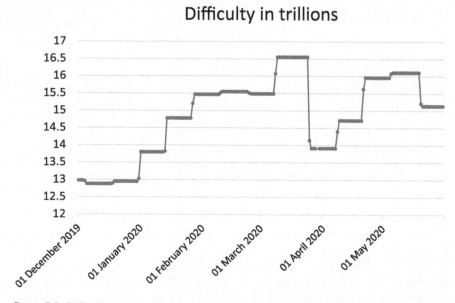

Figure 7.8 Difficulty.

Note: On the Bitcoin network, difficulty adjustments take place every 2016 blocks. That is about two weeks.

This may mean that miners can switch their machines back on again, though there will be miners who had to sell equipment and assets to cover the costs of buildings and other running costs. These miners will likely not have returned to mining once it became profitable and so these events can have an impact on who is mining.

The miner capitulation events caused by price drops ultimately resolve themselves, but the resultant drop in hash rate reduces security on the network and changes the balance of miners.

MINER CAPITULATION THROUGH COMPETITION

Miners can be caused to capitulate through being outcompeted on the network. As more hash power is added to the network, the block time decreases. This, in turn, leads to a difficulty adjustment to make it more difficult to mine a block. As their hash rate and electricity consumption is staying the same, but the frequency with which they mine a block and get the rewards for doing so decreases, they may become unprofitable and capitulate.

Normally this is caused by newer ASIC machines becoming available. As they provide higher hash rates per kilowatt of energy, they contribute a higher proportion of the hashing on the system.

When the first cryptocurrency Bitcoin was released, it was possible to mine with a regular computer and receive large amounts of cryptocurrency in return. As time went by, miners made mining units from systems with several graphics cards, as their GPUs were relatively efficient in processing hashes. When this happened, other systems on the network could not compete and it began to cost more to run the laptop mining Bitcoin than you would receive in return.

After this, dedicated mining units became available that were specially designed to be efficient at processing hashes. These machines are commonly known as Application Specific Integrated Circuit or ASIC for short. They, in turn, pushed most GPU-based mining rigs out of the marketplace and currently most mining is done by dedicated ASIC machines.

Those close to the new technology tend to win out by gaining access to the new tech more quickly and outcompeting the older machines, which have become less profitable. For this reason, China and the US are responsible for the majority of the hash power of the Bitcoin network. Cheap electricity costs also contribute to the success of China, in this regard.

Block height:	693119
Hash	0000000000000000000d332ea1218a533a0cdf5f39e8da4ec6993784581 54326
Date	29th July 2021
Time	10:56am
Confirmations	7
Size	1327 kB
Reward	6.25 BTC
Difficulty	13672594272814
Merkle root	23fc0e205f559841baf22bae49eddb9c24409bb0532726de325c9d9c90b0cfe2

Figure 7.9 Bitcoin block information.

MINING POOLS

When a miner guesses at nonces and is rewarded for their success, the time in between those successes can be long. With any given nodes chances of being the one to find a valid nonce being relatively small, one could conceivably mine for a long time and never make anything in return for doing it. Equally, as luck is involved, you might stumble upon a valid nonce very quickly. The rewards for doing mining a block can be high. In Bitcoin, for example, you receive at the time of writing 6.25 Bitcoin (around $60,250) as a block reward and the transaction fees for all the transactions in that block.

Here is a block from the Bitcoin blockchain. You can see the miner was rewarded over $60,000. Your chances of being the one to do this, however, are quite low and that is where mining pools come in. We used the analogy of a lottery earlier when we considered mining. If guessing a nonce is like a ticket to this lottery, where the prize is the block reward and transaction fee, then mining pools are like lottery syndicates. They are different miners working together to share hash power and the rewards they receive. They give the miners the ability to stabilize the income from their mining activities.

Many miners would not be able to operate without a mining pool. The distance between their wins would be too infrequent to compete with other miners. The mining pool spreads out these wins and allows miners who would otherwise not be able to compete, to mine.

Halving	Date	Block Height	Block Reward (BTC)
1	28th Nov /2012	210,000	25
2	9th July /2016	420,000	12.5
3	12th May /2020	630,000	6.25

Figure 7.10 The Bitcoin halving and rewards.

**Note: The last Bitcoin will should be mined in 2040 and will have a block reward of a single Satoshi

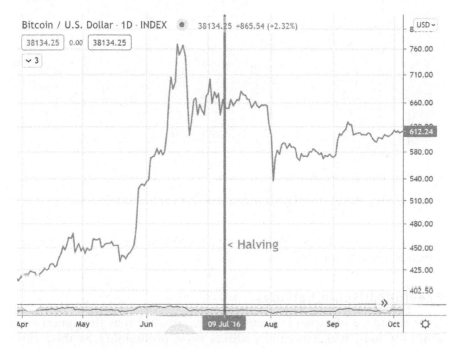

Figure 7.11 Bitcoin price at halving.

Source: Charting platform used for this analysis is provided by TradingView.

HALVINGS AND THE HALVENING

Another event that has similar effects on miners, hash rate and cryptocurrency values is commonly called both a halving and the halvening. Built into Bitcoin and many other cryptocurrencies is a mechanism to reduce and eventually eliminate inflation. We have seen how miners are rewarded, not just with transaction fees, but also with block rewards. In the beginning, the

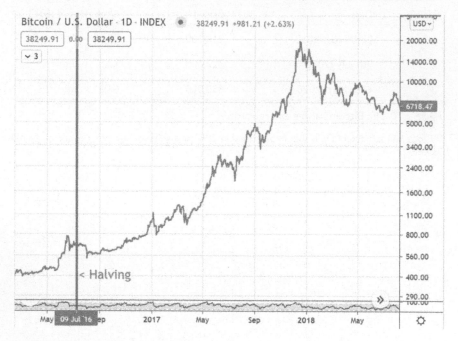

Figure 7.12 Bitcoin price after halving.

Source: Charting platform used for this analysis is provided by TradingView.

rewards were 50 BTC per block. Every 210,000 blocks that amount halves which is around four years.

Previous Bitcoin halvings

Over the space of around 10 minutes, the amount that the miners earn drops by half, which naturally affects their profitability as their costs remain the same. In this situation, a number of miners will capitulate and sell their coins. This increases sell pressure and the price of the cryptocurrency drops. This can be seen in the price chart below which shows the 2016 halving.

Once the capitulation was over, however, having gone through the same process as outlined before with the effect on the hash rate and corresponding changes in difficulty, the reduction in sell pressure ultimately resulted in a parabolic price increase for the cryptocurrency which can be seen below.

This result is what leads to the significance of the halving event and why it is eagerly anticipated by many cryptocurrency holders.

Key points about mining

- Mining power, for Proof of Work, is measured in Terahashes per second (TH/s).
- Miners can be caused to capitulate when the price drops or the block reward drops.
- This causes a drop in hash rate and an adjustment in the difficulty.
- Miners can also be caused to capitulate when they are out-powered by the other machines on the network.

REFERENCES

Bitinfocharts (2021) *Bitcoin Block Time historical chart* Available at https://bitinf ocharts.com/comparison/Bitcoin-confirmationtime.html#3y [Accessed 29 July 2021].

Bitmain (2021) *Antminer S19 Pro*. Available at: https://shop.bitmain.com/release/ AntminerS19Pro/overview [Accessed 28 July 2021].

Bitmain (2021 B) *Antminer Z15*. Available at: https://shop.bitmain.com/product/det ail?pid=00020210626152556693EcBT02pE0652 [Accessed 28 July 2021].

TradingView (2021) *TradingView*. Available at www.tradingview.com/chart [Accessed 28 July 2021].

Chapter 8

Summary of blockchain so far

IN THE PREVIOUS CHAPTERS

We have seen how hashing is used to timestamp blocks, which are linked together in sequence. Each block contains information. For cryptocurrencies this is transaction data.

We have seen how blockchain uses a web of decentralized nodes, each carrying a copy of the data and a pool of transactions waiting to be added to the blockchain, in a "mempool".

A diagram of all of these put together is shown over page.

In addition, we have looked at how public and private key cryptography is used to create and sign data, allowing us to create and use cryptocurrency wallets.

We have seen how forks can occur, both through mining and through updates and we have seen how these are resolved. We have discussed consensus mechanisms and considered the implications of the selection of a number of consensus mechanisms.

You should already have a good understanding of how blockchains function. In the coming sections we will expand on this by looking at Blockchain 2.0 and Distributed Applications, smart contracts and DApp development. We will talk about tokens and tokenization including Non-Fungible Tokens (NFTs) and stable coins. We will also discuss some of the privacy-based coins that attempt to obfuscate information available on the blockchain. We are also going to take a look at the types of attacks that are possible.

Key points summary

- Blockchains allow for trustless relationships.
- They have many applications including establishing provenance.
- They are resilient against issues with downtime.

DOI: 10.1201/9781003187165-8

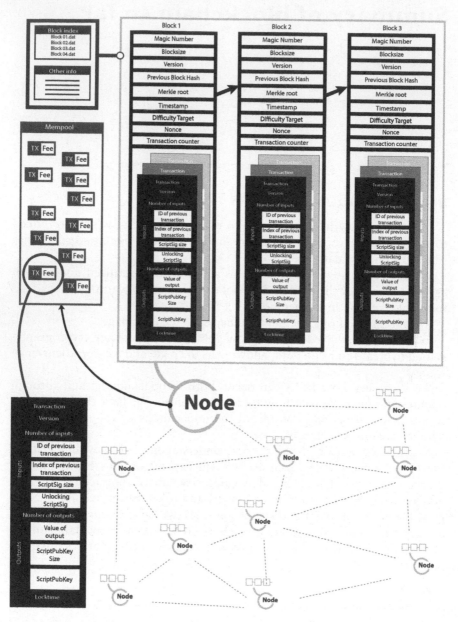

Figure 8.1 Blockchain summary.

blocks, together with metadata about the block.

- Once something is written into the blockchain it is very difficult or impossible to change.
- Blockchains make wide use of hashes and encryption to link blocks and allow for signatures to establish credentials.
- They typically contain a Merkle tree of hashes of the data contained in the block.
- The block's data is hashed to create a value.
- The block has a value called nonce which can be changed to change the resultant hash.
- There is a difficulty target value which the hash of the block must be below to be accepted.
- Blockchains are stored on a distributed network of computers. The nodes compare their copy of the blockchain with the copy on the other nodes.
- Nodes will switch to the longest version.
- The network uses the version of the blockchain that has had the most work done on it.
- The mechanism of using hash power to establish work done is called *Proof of Work*.
- Nodes can be full nodes or partial nodes. Partial nodes can consult full nodes if they need to.
- Distribution makes it difficult for anyone to take the network down.
- Accidental forks are caused when new blocks are found in multiple places on the network, before one version can be fully distributed across the network.
- Accidental forks will resolve themselves when one chain grows longer.
- Update forks occur when some systems update and others do not.
- Wallets are a public and private key pair where the public key is derived from the private key.
- The Private Key is used to sign transactions.
- The public key or derivatives of the public key are used to track and receive funds.
- Transactions are stored in blocks either as UTXOs or account balances.
- Consensus mechanisms allow the nodes on a network to agree on who is allowed to create the next block. They are a method of making sure that all nodes on the network agree and that they all act fairly.

- In Proof of Work (PoW) nodes take guesses at nonces to find a valid nonce to make the hash meet the hash target.
- In Proof of Stake (PoS) nodes "stake" tokens, their stake gives them a chance of being the next to create a block.

Chapter 9

Blockchain 2.0

The types of blockchain that we have looked at up until this point are what is widely referred to as blockchain 1.0. This is because they are very similar to the original blockchain Bitcoin, in their structure and function. Since these blockchains first arrived, there have been further developments, widely known as blockchain 2.0.

If you read the preface, you will recall that I compared blockchains to the internet in its infancy. To extend this analogy, if blockchain 1.0 is comparable to static web pages, blockchain 2.0 is comparable to the move to dynamic web pages and web applications. There is so much more possible with blockchain 2.0. Let's look at what the differences are and how it all works.

SMART CONTRACTS

The second era of blockchain was ushered in with the advent of Ethereum and its use of so-called *smart contracts* that allow developers to program money. *Smart contracts* are to blockchain what vending machines are to shops. They take a set transaction, a contract, and automate those parts that do not require human intervention. A vending machine equalizes everyone and adheres to the rules, no matter who is using it. It will not let its friends skip the queue or receive items for free. In the same way, a smart contract's code prevents exceptions from being made, it prevents outside tampering and corruption. Its code, once initiated, is practically unstoppable. We will look at how and why this is, in the coming section.

There are two parts to the smart contract system:

1. The smart contract: A piece or pieces of code that execute, moving coins/tokens between contracts and accounts.
2. The Virtual Machine: The part that executes the code on the nodes.

DOI: 10.1201/9781003187165-9

Smart contracts are code, typically written in a specialized language with key terms and variable types specifically for holding contract addresses and structures. That code is stored in the blockchain. The code is therefore immutable once added. It can execute using the virtual machine and it can conclude, but it cannot be erased and it cannot be stopped. Probably the most commonly used such language is Solidity.

Figure 9.1 shows a very basic "Hello World" Example in Solidity. We will not be going into programming smart contracts in this book, and I will not be going into the details of what the individual lines of code are doing. At this stage, however, it may be useful to understand what a smart contract looks like.

VIRTUAL MACHINES

Normally when a programmer writes code, the code is executed by a computer's Central Processing Unit (CPU). For regular applications, this is

```
1   /////////////////////////////////////////////
2   //  A Simple Hello World Example
3   //  Akira Summers
4   /////////////////////////////////////////////
5
6   // State version of solidity that we are using
7   pragma solidity 0.5.12;
8
9
10  // The contract
11  contract hiworld {
12
13    // a stored value within the contract
14    string message = "hello World";
15
16    // This function gets the message that is stored in the contract
17    function getMessage () public view returns(string memory){
18      return message;
19    }
20
21    // This function sets the message stored by the contract
22    function setMessage ( string memory newMessage) public payable{
23      message = newMessage;
24    }
25
26  }
```

Figure 9.1 Solidity code.

generally a reasonable thing to do. You have control over which applications run on your computer and once you allow a program to execute, those applications require the capacity to implement changes to the computers that they execute on, to write to the hard disk, delete files and generally have control over all aspects of what the computer can do. If you make a wrong choice, however, like allowing some malware to execute, the consequences can be grim.

With blockchain programming, this could result in very bad things happening. Anyone and everyone has access to public blockchains and so allowing them all to run whatever code they like directly could be a great security issue. For this reason, the code is not executed directly by the CPU, instead, it is run by a separate *virtual machine* that can ensure that nothing untoward happens when the code is executed. It can execute the code, while protecting the machine that it is running on.

The code that you write in languages such as Solidity is first processed into a form more readable by the virtual machine called *bytecode*. The bytecode is a representation of the same actions that the contract performs.

The code from the smart contract is added to the blockchain as bytecode and then executed when called on to do so. It has to be executed on each of the nodes and show that it has the same result on each of them for its actions, their inputs and outputs, to be considered valid by the network.

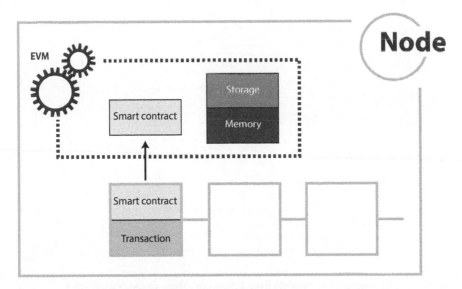

Figure 9.2 Ethereum Virtual Machine (EVM): An overview.

JUNK DATA, COMPUTATIONAL COSTS AND GAS

In an environment where anyone can add code to the blockchain and that code will be run on many systems, it would be easy for any reasonable programmer with nefarious intent to clog the system up with activities that kept it busy enough to prohibit it from processing "real" requests. To prevent this, there are a few different mechanisms that the different blockchain 2.0 solutions employ. The most widely known and used is that of the charging of a fee to process information. To upload and execute a smart contract, it is common to pay a "gas" fee.

Each different thing that the contract can do, from adding values or multiplying them to storing values for later use, has an associated gas fee, representing how much work it is to perform that action.

This is only really an issue for public blockchains, the large majority of which are cryptocurrencies. In private blockchains access to the network is

APPENDIX G. FEE SCHEDULE

The fee schedule G is a tuple of scalar values corresponding to the relative costs, in gas, of a number of abstract operations that a transaction may effect.

Name	Value	Description
G_{zero}	0	Nothing paid for operations of the set W_{zero}.
$G_{jumpdest}$	1	Amount of gas to pay for a JUMPDEST operation.
G_{base}	2	Amount of gas to pay for operations of the set W_{base}.
$G_{verylow}$	3	Amount of gas to pay for operations of the set $W_{verylow}$.
G_{low}	5	Amount of gas to pay for operations of the set W_{low}.
G_{mid}	8	Amount of gas to pay for operations of the set W_{mid}.
G_{high}	10	Amount of gas to pay for operations of the set W_{high}.
$G_{extcode}$	700	Amount of gas to pay for operations of the set $W_{extcode}$.
$G_{balance}$	700	Amount of gas to pay for a BALANCE operation.
G_{sload}	800	Paid for an SLOAD operation.
G_{sset}	20000	Paid for an SSTORE operation when the storage value is set to non-zero from zero.
G_{sreset}	5000	Paid for an SSTORE operation when the storage value's zeroness remains unchanged or is set to zero.
R_{sclear}	15000	Refund given (added into refund counter) when the storage value is set to zero from non-zero.
$R_{selfdestruct}$	24000	Refund given (added into refund counter) for self-destructing an account.
$G_{selfdestruct}$	5000	Amount of gas to pay for a SELFDESTRUCT operation.
G_{create}	32000	Paid for a CREATE operation.
$G_{codedeposit}$	200	Paid per byte for a CREATE operation to succeed in placing code into state.
G_{call}	700	Paid for a CALL operation.
$G_{callvalue}$	9000	Paid for a non-zero value transfer as part of the CALL operation.
$G_{callstipend}$	2300	A stipend for the called contract subtracted from $G_{callvalue}$ for a non-zero value transfer.
$G_{newaccount}$	25000	Paid for a CALL or SELFDESTRUCT operation which creates an account.
G_{exp}	10	Partial payment for an EXP operation.
$G_{expbyte}$	50	Partial payment when multiplied by the number of bytes in the exponent for the EXP operation.
G_{memory}	3	Paid for every additional word when expanding memory.
$G_{txcreate}$	32000	Paid by all contract-creating transactions after the $Homestead$ transition.
$G_{txdatazero}$	4	Paid for every zero byte of data or code for a transaction.
$G_{txdatanonzero}$	16	Paid for every non-zero byte of data or code for a transaction.
$G_{transaction}$	21000	Paid for every transaction.
G_{log}	375	Partial payment for a LOG operation.
$G_{logdata}$	8	Paid for each byte in a LOG operation's data.
$G_{logtopic}$	375	Paid for each topic of a LOG operation.
G_{sha3}	30	Paid for each SHA3 operation.
$G_{sha3word}$	6	Paid for each word (rounded up) for input data to a SHA3 operation.
G_{copy}	3	Partial payment for *COPY operations, multiplied by words copied, rounded up.
$G_{blockhash}$	20	Payment for BLOCKHASH operation.
$G_{quaddivisor}$	20	The quadratic coefficient of the input sizes of the exponentiation-over-modulo precompiled contract.

Figure 9.3 Ethereum gas fee schedule from Ethereum yellow paper (Wood 2014).

Printed with kind permission of the Ethereum yellow paper author, Dr. Gavin Wood.

managed and so malicious nodes can be removed. We will discuss private blockchains in more detail in the following section.

In these networks, gas is separate to the cryptocurrency of the network that it operates on. Though that gas fee is converted and normally ultimately charged in the currency of the network, there is a conversion between the two that can be varied. The reason for this being that as the price of the cryptocurrency varies, it would affect the cost of performing the transactions. Should the cryptocurrency go up 1000 per cent in price, you wouldn't want the cost of executing a transfer between contracts to go up 1000 per cent also. This would have great implications for how cost-effective it would be to make use of smart contracts. Instead, there is a conversion between the gas price and the currency.

This is the chart of the gas price in Gwei (a division of ether, the Ethereum coin) from the Ethereum network, over the past few years. You can see that the price in gas has fluctuated. The price should decrease as the price of ether has gone up over the same period, but the price also responds to demands on the network, with gas prices increasing at times of greater congestion.

So, the use of gas is a mechanism to stop the network from being clogged up with junk information, by making it expensive to do so. It is not the only idea for doing so though. The cryptocurrency Tron uses "energy" and "bandwidth" to pay for processing, which you receive in return for staking on the network. This also makes filling up the network with junk costly as

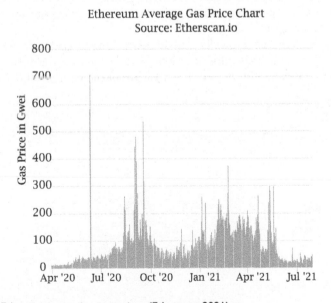

Figure 9.4 Ethereum gas price over time (Etherscan 2021).

Excerpt from Etherscan.io available at https://etherscan.io/chart/gasprice.

you have to stake large amounts to add large amounts of data, but it does not use up the currency.

DAPPS

DApps are **D**istributed **A**pplication. Here are the criteria for something to be considered a DApp that you will commonly see:

1. Open Source – Source code of the app is available to all.
2. Decentralized – Uses a blockchain-like cryptographic technology.
3. Incentive – App has crypto-tokens/digital assets for fuelling itself.
4. Algorithm/Protocol – Generates tokens and has an inbuilt consensus mechanism.

Technically, under these conditions, most cryptocurrencies would be considered to be DApps. Normally though when people use the term DApp, they are referring to applications that interact with the blockchain and this is the definition we will work with below.

We have already discussed how code can execute on the blockchain using bytecode, stored in the blockchain and executed by a virtual machine. These form the first part of a DApp. The other part comes in the form of the interface. This could be in the form of a front-end like a web page, mobile phone app or a computer application. It could also be through an interface with another application such as an exchange. Though definitions of this vary a little, generally we can consider to the DApp to be the combination of the smart contract and the interface.

The interfaces are typically linked with library code, which provides standard functions that allow the interface to operate the functionality of the smart contract. This arrangement is shown in the following diagram.

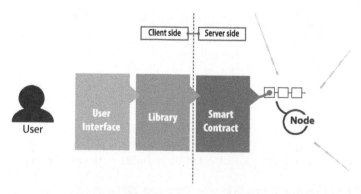

Figure 9.5 Example of a DApp structure.

Given that blockchains largely deal with asset management in some form, DApps are typically designed and created to manage money or assets. Common applications include distributed exchanges for exchanging, staking and managing cryptocurrencies and gambling. Use cases are developing with time and novel applications are appearing and growing.

Figure 9.6 shows an example of code that runs on a web page (shown on the right), that connects to the smart contract and inserts that information into the HTML of the page, using JavaScript (shown on the left).

DApps are typically integrated with one or more smart contracts. They might, for example, allow for several people to take funds from their wallet and pay it into a contract balance. The interest of that balance might then be randomly awarded to one of the contributors as a non-cost lottery. The accounts, the balances and other aspects are managed automatically by the smart contract. The user will interface with the front-end of the DApp, probably through a web page and the code executes in the blockchain, the results of this are available for all to see and verify.

In the example above the smart contract would likely interact with a single blockchain. They can, however, work across several blockchains. They can pull information from outside sources via an oracle server. These are servers that can provide external information such as prices of cryptocurrency stocks, weather or any other desired values.

Summary of DApp structure

The code of the DApp, from the front-end and the back-end, is completely visible to everyone who cares to look into the content of the blockchain and the source of the web page (fig 9.7). Security is, therefore, of utmost concern. Several hacks have taken place where vulnerabilities in the code have been found and exploited.

SMART CONTRACTS VULNERABILITIES AND SECURITY

Development of smart contracts requires careful attention to security. The reasons for this are three-fold.

1. They handle lots of money, which makes them tempting targets when compared to other software.
2. The code is publicly viewable, as it resides on an open blockchain.
3. The code is immutable, once it is written to the blockchain, it cannot be changed. There are methods to make values editable and therefore change some parts of the execution, otherwise, it would not be practical to have code on the blockchain, but the code itself remains the same.

```
main.js
1  var web3 = new Web3(Web3.givenProvider);
2  var contractInstance;
3  var contractAddress = "0x85d7122496dE5629B9330049Af428131E
4  var winState;
5  var gameStake;

   $(document).ready(function() {
     window.ethereum.enable().then(function(accounts){
       contractInstance = new web3.eth.Contract(abi, contra
       console.log("contract instance was ");
       console.log(contractInstance);
     });
     setStake();
     updatestake();
     $("#winlose").text("You have not played yet!");
     $("#setStake").click(setStake);
     $("#play").click(playTheGame);
   });

   // gets data from form
   async function playTheGame(){
   // play the gameplay
```

```
index.html
1  <!DOCTYPE html>
2  <html>
   <head>
     <meta charset="utf-8">
     <meta name="viewport" content="width=device-width, ini
     <title>Crypto Gaming</title>
     <script src="https://code.jquery.com/jquery-3.4.1.min
       integrity="sha256-CSXorXvZcTkaix6YvoGHppcZGEtbYNGWSF
       crossorigin="anonymous"></script>
     <script type="text/javascript" src="./web3.min.js"></s
     <script type="text/javascript" src="./abi.js"></script
     <script type="text/javascript" src="./main.js"></scri
     <script src="https://stackpath.bootstrapcdn.com/bootst
     <link rel="stylesheet" href="https://stackpath.bootstr
   </head>
   <body>
     <div class="jumbotron jumbotron-fluid">
       <div class="container">
         <h1 class="display-4">Casino Game</h1>
22       <p class="lead">Spin the wheel] - win some coins! <
       </div>
24     </div>
     <div class="container">
       <h2>How dangerous are you?</h2>
```

Figure 9.6 Example DApp code.

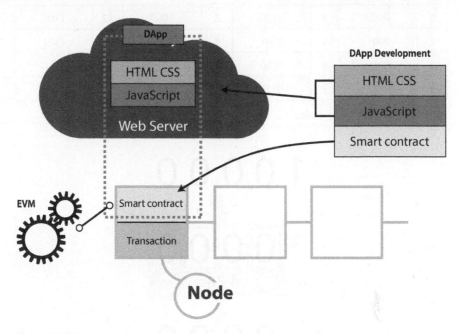

Figure 9.7 DApp structure.

Things are complicated further by the fact that contracts do not just interact with people, they interact with other contracts and other code that accesses the contracts. These issues have led to several exploits. We will look at a couple of the most significant.

Overflow

Overflow exploits are used in various places in computing and manifest in different ways. The basic principle is that a value larger than the largest storable value is stored, which causes the computer to misbehave. Let's look at how this works in smart contracts.

A computer value is stored in binary, using a certain number of bits. Though the number of bits we work with in smart contracts is significantly higher, to keep this example simple, let's say we have only four bits to store the values. We can store the following values (fig 9.8).

So, what happens if we try and store the value 16? That would be 10000 in binary, but we can only store four bits, so we lose the leading one and end up with 0000.

0	0000	4	0100	8	1000	12	1100
1	0001	5	0101	9	1001	13	1101
2	0010	6	0110	10	1010	14	1110
3	0011	7	0111	11	1011	15	1111

Figure 9.8 Table of binary codes.

Figure 9.9 Overflow error.

This is an overflow. Let's look at how it has been used to exploit a smart contract. Possibly the most commonly known example of this is from BeautyChain, where a function transferred from one wallet to several people's wallets.

The function worked something like this pseudo code example, where I have added comments on lines starting with // to tell you what is happening:

```
// this function receives the number of people to
pay // and the amount to pay them

Function PayoutToMultipleAccounts (NumberOfPayees,
AmountToPay)

    // the TotalToPayout is NumberOfPayees multiplied
    by AmountToPay TotalToPayout = NumberOfPayees
    * AmountToPay ;

    // Check that the account has enough to cover
    to  total  cost  CheckAccountHasEnoughToPay
    ( TotalToPayout ) ;
```

```
ForEachPayee {

    // transfer them the amount to payout
    TransferToPayee ( AmountToPay );

}

// then remove the total cost from the account
DeductFromBalance ( TotalToPayout ) ;
```

This is not actual code from a smart contract, instead it is a simplified version, to show more clearly what happens. What it is doing is adding up all the payments to be sent and checking this is less than the value of the account holder's balance. Let's run through this example using our three bits from above. Imagine we are sending four coins to two accounts. That would make eight coins in total being paid out.

```
Function PayoutToMultipleAccounts (NumberOfPayees=
2, AmountToPay=4)

    // the TotalToPayout is 8 TotalToPayout =
    NumberOfPayees * AmountToPay ;

    // Check that the account has enough to cover
    to total cost of 8 CheckAccountHasEnoughToPay
    ( TotalToPayout ) ;

ForEachPayee {

    // transfer them each 4 coins TransferToPayee
    ( AmountToPay );

}

// then remove the total cost of 8 coins from the
account DeductFromBalance ( TotalToPayout ) ;
```

This works very well. What happens if we enter a value large enough to overflow though? Let's go through again and imagine we are paying out eight coins to two accounts and that we are using four bits to store the values.

```
Function PayoutToMultipleAccounts (NumberOfPayees=
2, AmountToPay=8)

    // the TotalToPayout is 16, but overflows,
    so is zero. // The AmountToPay is still
    8. TotalToPayout = NumberOfPayees * AmountToPay ;
```

```
    // Check that the account has enough to cover to
    total cost of zero coins

    CheckAccountHasEnoughToPay ( TotalToPayout ) ;

    ForEachPayee {

            // transfer them each 8 coins
            TransferToPayee ( AmountToPay );

    }

    // then remove the total cost of zero coins from
    the account DeductFromBalance ( TotalToPayout )
```

We can see that the checks work well unless the overflow is reached. If the number overflows, it passes the checks, pays out the larger sum and then removes nothing from the account balance. We only used four bits to make the example easy, giving us a maximum value of 15. In smart contracts, the number of bits and the maximum numbers are much higher.

In the case of BeautyChain, this allowed a hacker to transfer very large numbers of tokens from the contract. So how do we cope with this? We can use some checks to make sure that the calculation works as desired. Rather than the problematic line

```
    TotalToPayout = NumberOfPayees * AmountToPay ;
```

we can instead add numbers together using a function that performs some checks on the outputs. These checks, commonly called "sanity checks", ensure that the outputs are reasonable.

That function might look something like this:

```
    // multiplies two values and checks the result
    Function SafeMultiply (ValueA, ValueB)
            Result = ValueA * ValueB;
            CheckThat ( ValueB = Result/ValueA ); // check
            by dividing
            SendBack Result;
    }
```

This function applies the multiplication, then checks that it works, by dividing it again and checking the value, otherwise it will throw an error and stop. Our problematic line can be fixed by swapping it then to:

```
    TotalToPayout = SafeMultiply (NumberOfPayees,
                    AmountToPay) ;
```

There are libraries of functions we can use to develop our code, which already has these checks built into them, such as the SafeMaths Library.

Another thing that we can do is to use unit testing. This allows us to write a test for each of our functions, calling them with a range of different values and check the output to make sure it is in-line with what we expect. This helps us to identify and resolve issues before they are written to the blockchain.

Re-entrancy attack

This type of vulnerability works by stopping and re-entering a program. By selecting where this happens, you can influence the way a function works. You can see examples of this outside of smart contracts.

Consider a fruit machine with reels that roll when the button is pressed. If we wait for them to stop, then take the stake and test whether a winning combination is present, a savvy player might switch the machine off when the first two reels have stopped if they didn't like the look of them, then replay with the same money after.

This works much the same way in a smart contract. Imagine we have a function that pays out the balance of a user's account to them, then clears the amount of their balance. This might look something like this:

```
Function Payout{
     withdraw ( amount );
     balance = balance - amount;
     }
```

If we are calling this with another contract, it is possible to stop this function and run it again after it has executed the first line. This will cause it to enter into a loop of paying out but not resetting the recorded account balance, re-entering the function again and again, without completing.

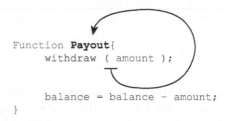

Figure 9.10 Re-entrancy.

The most commonly known instance of this attack in smart contracts was the DAO attack, where this exploit was used to steal $70,000,000 of Ether. The solution is, however, rather simple. We should always adjust the account balance before paying out. In general, we should always update the value before performing interactions.

> Note: After the DAO Hack the Ethereum blockchain was reverted to a time before the attack. Not everyone agreed with this which resulted in a Fork of the Ethereum network.

Though there are other examples of vulnerabilities, these should give you an idea of the complexity of issues and consequences of such issues.

Key points about smart contracts and DApps

- They allow developers to program money
- There are two parts to the smart contract system:
  - The smart contract – A piece or pieces of code that execute, moving coins/tokens between contracts and accounts.
  - The Virtual Machine – The part that executes the code on the nodes.
- The smart contract is stored in the blockchain.
- Before being stored on the blockchain, they are first processed into a form more readable by the virtual machine called *bytecode*.
- To upload and execute a smart contract, it is common to pay a "gas" fee.
- DApps are Distributed Applications.
- DApps typically integrate with one or more smart contracts.
- Development of smart contracts requires careful attention to security.
- Overflow exploits allow malicious changes to values by creating values larger than the value can store.
- Re-entrancy attacks work by stopping and re-entering a function

---

TESTNETS

When developers work on DApp projects typically they will wish to avoid paying the gas cost or similar to cover the cost of running testing on the system as it is developing. In a similar manner to web developers who work first on local servers, they instead work on test networks. These are identical to the mainnet in function, but the currency that they hold is given away freely and is therefore not saleable. One such testnet is Ethereum's Ropsten Network. With this network, DApps can be freely deployed and tested with ether obtained from a *faucet*. A faucet is a term given to a free source of Ethereum tokens, for the testnet.

Besides the lack of charges for currency and the different content on the chain, testnets are in all other senses a replica of the mainnet. Blocks are mined in the same manner and transactions and code are added as new blocks are mined and executed by the Virtual Machine when called on to do so.

Testnets also allow for the development of the blockchain code itself. Any changes to the functionality of the blockchain can be deployed as a testnet and its operation monitored, to ensure it is operating within desired parameters.

LOCAL TESTING

Sometimes working with a testnet is not fast enough for the developer. If you are writing a piece of code, you often want to quickly establish if it is working, without the need to deploy it to the testnet and wait for

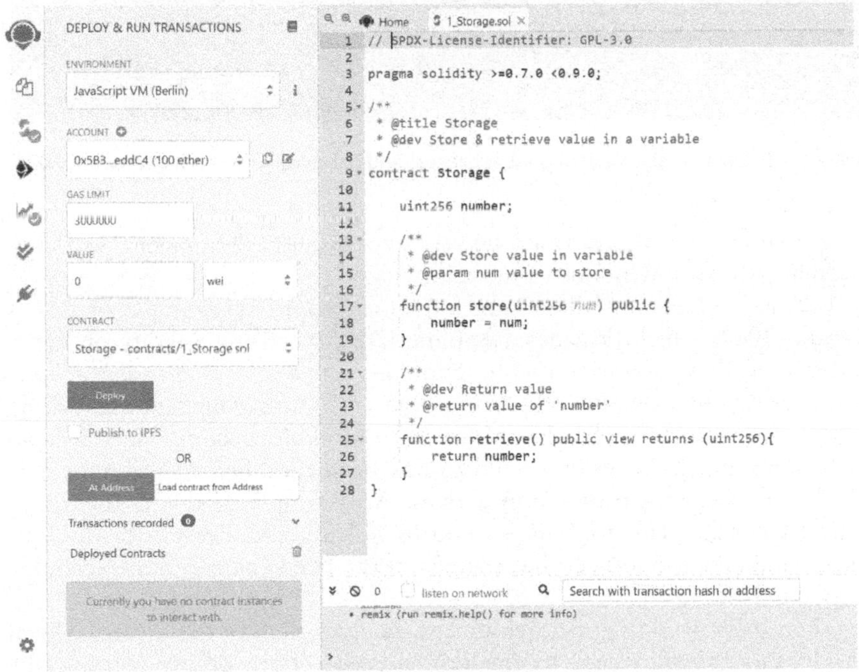

Figure 9.11 Remix IDE editing a Solidity file (Remix 2021).

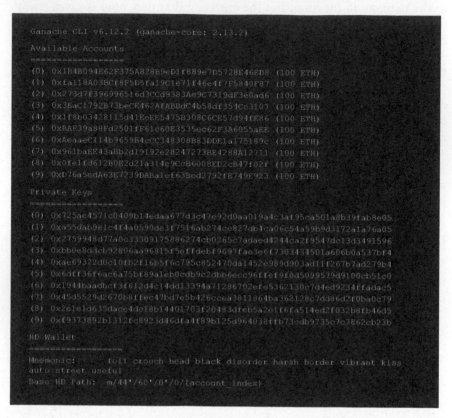

Figure 9.12 Ganache showing account addresses and balances (ConsenSys Software 2021).

confirmations. For this reason, the first step in the development of a DApp is usually to work with one of the following:

A Virtual Machine that simulates a blockchain. An example of this is Remix (2021) which provides an online IDE for writing Solidity or Vyper code, then allows you to test its functionality using a *Java Virtual Machine.*

A modified blockchain on your computer. We can circumvent the waiting process for mining new blocks by running a local blockchain, which instead of hashing blocks to establish PoW, has been modified to generate new blocks every time a transaction arrives. An example of this is the application Ganache. This tool allows you to quickly add a test code on your local computer and inspect the contents of the blockchain and the accounts associated with it.

Often the workflow for development includes each of these stages, local development, deployment to the testnet and then progression onto the mainnet.

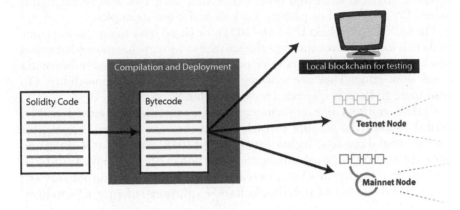

Figure 9.13 A common development process for smart contracts using the Truffle suite.

Whether you are working on a local blockchain like Ganache, a testnet or the mainnet, you will also need to compile your contracts before deploying them. This will take the code that you have written and transform it into the bytecode required by the blockchains Virtual Machine that executes the code. For Ethereum, this is often done through Truffle which is a framework of command-line tools that assist with compilation, testing and deployment, taking the code and adding it to the blockchain.

Key points about development

- Testing and development is usually done on a simulated blockchain or a local modified blockchain.
- Code is then usually deployed or migrated to a test server, which is the same as the main server but with free tokens.
- Common tools for development include Ganache and truffle.

TOKENIZATION

The cryptocurrencies that we have discussed have transacted coins. It is also possible to create tokens on top of some cryptocurrencies. In addition to the cryptocurrency of the network, you can create your own tokens that are perhaps linked to concepts and items in the real world. A token is tradable in the same manner and can represent a variety of things.

Tokens can be fungible assets like stocks and shares, they could be non-fungible assets like houses or collectable items in games – a sword with a certain strength value and other properties. They can also be intangible assets, like copyrights or patents. Let's look at a few examples:

The CCEG Blockchain UN Lab (2021) for Good have many projects: one of them is looking at tokenizing values, in the same way that money tokenizes work. Think of all the socially responsible values that we have beyond a good work ethic. They are working to tokenize social responsibility. (To read more go here: https://ccegblockchain.com/)

Carbon emitters like governments and companies are issued carbon credits to limit the amount of carbon that they are allowed to emit, for environmental reasons. Technology Review (2018) report that Vedium and IBM are working on a tokenizing those carbon credits, to make trading of them more transparent. (You can read more here: www.technologyreview. com/2018/07/19/141404/blockchain-explainer-tokenizing-carbon-credits/.)

Different tokens can have their own rules for the minting (creation) of new coins and the burning (destruction) of coins. This can affect their scarcity and therefore real-world cost. When a token type has a mechanism that burns token on given events, the supply of those tokens goes down. As they become scarcer, their value increases.

One of the biggest developments in the tokenizing of assets was the development of standards. By using standards for tokens, we enable wallets and applications to work with those tokens more easily. Any token built on these standards is therefore automatically tradable by any application that utilizes that standard, without modification for each new token.

Ethereum has provided one such standard for fungible tokens called ERC20. It provides a standardized approach to transferring tokens and accessing data. This means that nearly every wallet that supports Ethereum will also support tokens made with the ERC20 standard. This makes it easy for you to conceive of a new concept for tokens and implement it without the need for a spate blockchain and adoption from wallets. You can easily create a token and begin writing DApps to interact with that token.

Ethereum has also provided standards for non-fungible tokens or NFTs such as ERC721 and ERC1155 tokens, where non-fungible items can be transferred and traded. An example of this is the game CyproKitties (Axiom Zen 2021), where you breed your own digital and unique cats. You can then buy, sell and trade them as collectables.

CryptoKitties are collectible and breedable digital cats. It's the world's first game built on the Ethereum network. When two CryptoKitties breed, their offspring's appearance and cattributes are determined by each parent's 256-bit genome and an element of chance, leading to 4-billion possible genetic variations.

CryptoKitties was created to explore the concept of digital scarcity, implement a non-fungible token within smart contracts ERC #721, and make blockchain technology accessible to everyday consumers.

(Axiom Zen 2021)

NFTs are not just used for game-based assets. NFTs allows you to tokenize real-world assets such as precious metals, real estate and other items. They are, in essence, tokens backed by real-world assets. One key issue with the use of real-world backed tokens is that there is very little regulation around their proof of ownership, so the legal position is often unclear if you buy a tokenized house, say, and the owner does not transfer ownership.

STABLE COINS

Probably the most commonly occurring fungible tokenized real-world assets are stable coins. With the desire of allowing cryptocurrency users to keep their assets in crypto to avoid the higher rate of transfer fees between crypto and fiat currency, an ERC20 token was created that was backed by the US Dollar called Tether. There are other similarly backed tokens for other fiat currencies like the British Pound and Australian and Canadian dollars.

There are some criticisms of tokens backed by real-world fiat currencies and their effect on centralization. By having a single organization that backs the asset with dollars, we add a significant element of centralization.

There are also stable coins that do not use this real-world backing to achieve stability at a level comparable to the dollar or other fiat currency such as Dai. As it does not require a centralized source of real-world assets backing it, Dai is a decentralized stable coin.

Dai achieves this by collateralizing cryptocurrency assets, denominated in dollars into what is known as a *collateralized debt position* or CDP. That is to say, to receive $100 of Dai, you would need to provide the appropriate amount of collateral in another asset. Let's see an example.

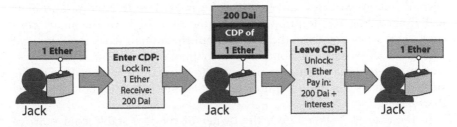

Figure 9.14 Dai CDP.

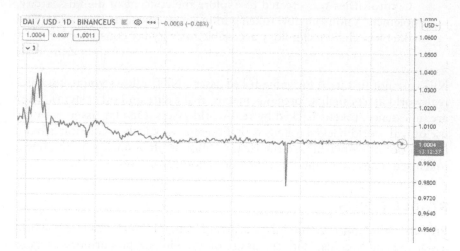

Figure 9.15 Dai price over time.

Source: Charting platform used for this analysis is provided by TradingView.

This shows Jack entering and leaving a collateralized debt position in Dai. In this example, it is assumed that the price of Dai is $200 at the time of entering the position. It does not matter how much it is worth at the end of the position, Jack simply pays back what he received, plus a little interest.

By minting new Dai, equivalent to the dollar value of the assets provided, and only releasing the asset back to the owner when they return the Dai, they can keep the value of the Dai coins stabilized at around $1.

DECENTRALIZED AUTONOMOUS ORGANIZATIONS (DAOS)

One interesting development that DApps and blockchains allow for is the creation of *decentralized autonomous organizations* or DAOs. Whereas traditional organizations deal with contracts and agreements, which are carried out by workers and enforced by laws, DAOs operate automatically, according to the programming, rules and logic of the smart contract. This saves greatly in the cost of all of the human work involved and allows for all work to be done without human intervention. If the organization meets these criteria, then it can be considered to be a DAO. The smart contracts operate the purchases, sales and transfers, completely by themselves.

In the case of Maker DAO, the owner of the Dai stable coin that we discussed earlier, it automatically receives assets, issues Dai, controls interest paid on the Dai received and returns the asset when the debt has been repaid.

Key points about tokenization and DAOs

- Pretty much anything can be tokenized.
- Token standards exist to make tokenizing easier and more compatible, including Ethereum's Fungible token standard ERC20 and non-fungible standards ERC721 and ERC1155.
- Stable coins can be created in a variety of ways, including tokenizing real-world coins.
- DAOs are decentralized autonomous organizations that use programmable money to create organizations that do not require human input to run.

REFERENCES

Axiom Zen (2021) *CryptoKitties* Available at www.cryptokitties.co/ [Accessed 28 July 2021].

CCEG Blockchain (2021) *CCEG Blockchain UN Lab.* Available at https://ccegblockchain.com/ [Accessed 28 July 2021].

ConsenSys Software (2021) Ganache (2.5.4). [computer software] Available through www.trufflesuite.com/ganache [Accessed 28 July 2021].

Etherscan (2021) *Ethereum Average Gas Price Chart* Available from https://etherscan.io/chart/gasprice [Accessed 29 July 2021].

Remix (2021) *Remix IDE.* Available at https://remix.ethereum.org/ [Accessed 28 July 2021].

Technology Review (2018) *IBM thinks blockchains can help reduce carbon emissions.* Available at www.technologyreview.com/2018/07/19/141404/blockchain-explainer-tokenizing-carbon-credits/ [Accessed 28 July 2021].

TradingView (2021) *TradingView.* Available at www.tradingview.com/chart [Accessed 28 July 2021].

Wood (2014) *Ethereum Yellow Paper.* Available at https://github.com/ethereum/yellowpaper [Accessed 28 July 2021].

Chapter 10

Public and private blockchains

So far, we have looked primarily at *public blockchains*. That is to say that everyone can access them. Anyone can decide to run a node or set up a wallet and begin interacting with it. Because you do not need permission to do this, *private blockchains* are also called *permissionless blockchains*.

There are instances, however, where you might not want everyone to have access to the content of the blockchain. Some corporate applications of blockchains, for example, might have a requirement that the contents are only shared among a selected group of peers. These *private blockchains* are also known as *permissioned blockchains*.

Figure 10.1 demonstrates why one might want to use a permissioned blockchain for supply chain management.

What this diagram is showing is that by using blockchain to enable multiple different organizations to share data, we replace often complex and varied systems, with sometimes contradictory information, with a secure method of interacting with a single unified version of the truth.

Currently, Hyperledger implementations account for the majority of permissioned blockchains and so we will focus on this in our explanations, though other permissioned blockchains work in very similar manners. Hyperledger is an open-source blockchain framework and associated tools and libraries. There are several different Hyperledger projects that have taken the Hyperledger framework and tuned to suit different purposes. Hyperledger projects can adopt a modular approach that allows developers to select from various options such as consensus mechanism and allows easy adaptation of block and transaction structure to create new *Distributed Ledger Technologies* (DLT).

A distributed ledger technology or DLT is a ledger, a list of ownership or registry that is distributed across a network. It does not need to be blockchain-based, though, in the context of blockchain, DLT is often used as a synonym for blockchain, particularly in permissioned systems.

The two most commonly known and used Hyperledger projects are Intel's Hyperledger Sawtooth and IBM maintained Hyperledger Fabric. Each is

DOI: 10.1201/9781003187165-10

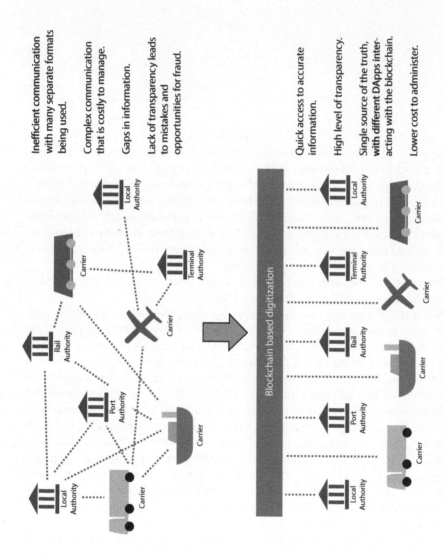

Inefficient communication with many separate formats being used.

Complex communication that is costly to manage.

Gaps in information.

Lack of transparency leads to mistakes and opportunities for fraud.

Quick access to accurate information.

High level of transparency.

Single source of the truth, with different DApps interacting with the blockchain.

Lower cost to administer.

Figure 10.1 Move to a blockchain-based supply chain.

built on the open-source code of Hyperledger but has its own properties. We use the terminology and processes outlined in the Hyperledger Fabric documentation (Hyperledger 2020) as a basis for the methods described this chapter, provided under creative commons (Creative Commons 2013).

One unique feature of Hyperledger Fabric is its ability to support different channels. Each channel is like a subnet of the network with its own ledger. It allows for a selected group of members to share information without making it available to the wider group. This has clear benefits in a corporate setting. More on channels in a moment.

Sawtooth includes Intel's consensus algorithm Proof of Elapsed Time and allows developers to select between this or Practical Byzantine Fault Tolerance. As PoET allows for nodes to "wake up" when their timers go off and become active, its inclusion allows for large numbers of validators with a lower level of resource consumption.

Blockchain projects often have different terminology for components and concepts such as nodes and staking. In Hyperledger and permissioned blockchains it is common to refer to nodes as peers, smart contracts as chain code, the blockchain as a ledger and the collective peers as a consortium and so we shall too, for this section.

CERTIFICATION AND PKI

The most important difference between permissioned blockchains is the restriction on who can access the network. There are other differences that result from this and others that result from what kinds of applications they tend to be adopted for, but determining who is allowed to read and write to the ledger is the one thing that defines a permissioned blockchain. This is achieved through a system known as Public Key Infrastructure or PKI.

PKI revolves around certificates generated using public and private keys, which contain their levels of access. There are four key aspects to a PKI:

1. Digital Certificates
2. Public and Private Keys
3. Certificate Authorities
4. Certificate Revocation Lists.

Overview

The identity is established through the use of a certificate, which we will look at in a moment. The identity, together with information about its accesses permissions and other information, such as which organization it is part of, are referred to as a principle.

Digital certificates are built on the concept of public and private key cryptography that we discussed earlier in this book. We have already discussed

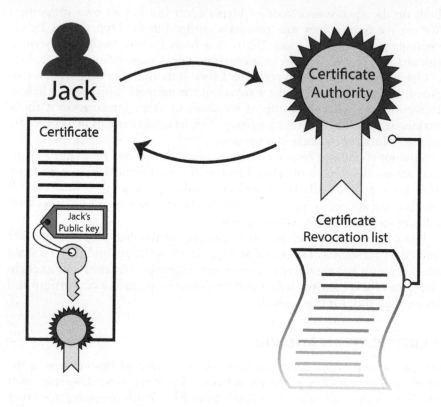

Figure 10.2 Certificate issuance in permissioned blockchains.

how public and private keys can be used to both encrypt information and sign information so that we can determine its origin.

Digital certificates are issued based on this through a certificate authority (CA) and access to the ledger is checked through the use of a Membership Service Provider or MSP, which checks principles before allowing reading or writing. Currently, the most commonly used certification in permissioned blockchain networks is the X509 standard.

Each CA will have a Certificate Revocation List (CRL) which lists certificates that are no longer valid. Certificates can be revoked for many reasons, such as breaches in security or organizations leaving the consortium.

DIGITAL CERTIFICATES

Let's look at an example taken. Here we see the certificate of the subject, "Jack". We can see key pieces of information about the certificate, including

Figure 10.3 An example certificate for Jack Jackson.

its serial number, the issuer and the period for which it is valid. We can also see key information about the subject including, their name, user ID, country, division and other pertinent information. Lastly, it includes the subject's public key. This matches the certificate owner's private key.

The combination of the certificate and the public/private key combination allows the certificated user to establish their credentials, so long as the certificate issuer is trusted. In this way, it acts as an ID card for access to the network.

CERTIFICATE AUTHORITIES

As we have seen, peers on the network are certificated to determine their level of access and their rights on the network. Those certificates are issued by an authority trusted by the system known as a certificate authority or CA. Those certificates are cryptographically validated and the most common standard for this is the X509 standard.

Figure 10.4 shows the certificate authority issuing certificates and the corresponding public and private keys.

These certificates issued to peers are digitally signed by the CA, whose public key is widely known and so certificates produced by the CA can be verified as originating from that source. The CA and the certificates issued link the peer with their public key and other relevant properties. So long as each of the participating organizations trusts the CA, then they can have trust in the certificates and credentials of the peers who receive them.

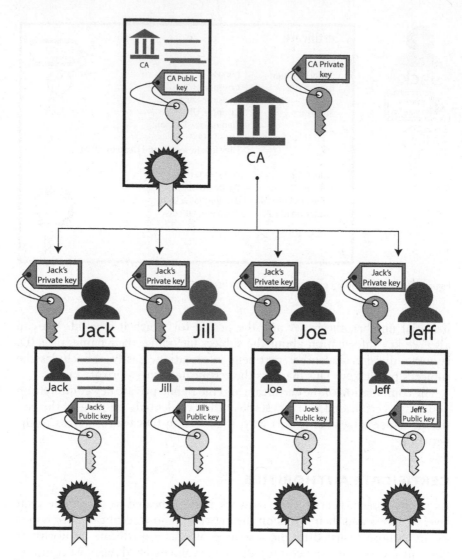

Figure 10.4 Certificates issued by CA.

The certificates themselves can be shared as they only contain public key rather than private key information. The private key is kept secure by the peer and can be used to sign and verify identity.

Because the blockchain is permissioned, every peer on the network will need a digital certificate to participate in any way. Typically, each organization that participates in the blockchain network will have its own CA so that it can issue certificates to new peers.

ROOT CERTIFICATE AUTHORITIES (RCAS) AND INTERMEDIATE CERTIFICATE AUTHORITIES (ICAS)

In any trans-organizational blockchain network, there are multiple CAs. This is because it would not be logical for only one organization to be in control of which peers are allowed to join the network. Instead, many CAs will have to work together to authenticate the peers on the network. In this situation, there is a Root Certification Authority or RCA that signs the certificates of the Intermediate Certificate Authorities or ICAs. These ICAs can then sign further ICA certificates of their own, creating chains of ICAs. These create what is referred to as Chains of Trust.

Chains of trust are useful not just to allow the creation of new ICAs, providing organizations with the capacity to manage their peers, they also increase the security of the network, but removing the need for the RCA to be on "active duty". If an ICA is compromised, re-establishing a replacement ICA is a much smaller issue than replacing the entire chain, should the RCA be compromised.

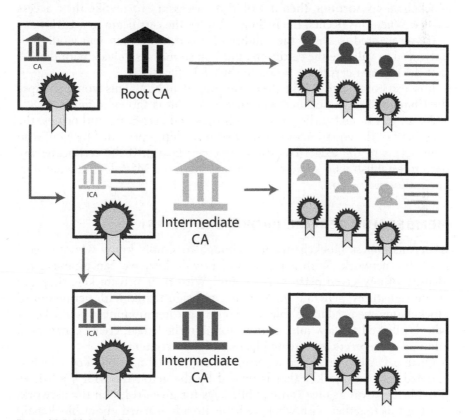

Figure 10.5 Multiple CAs.

Figure 10.5 shows the issuance of ICA certificates by the RCA and the ICA issuing its own certificates, both to individuals as well as another certificate authority. This creates Chains of Trust.

The PKI system and the use of RCAs and ICAs allows a great deal of flexibility in its application. It allows for a single RCA to sign and create ICAs as shown above or several RCAs to each sign and create their own ICAs, according to the requirements of the network and the various participating organizations.

Figure 10.6 shows an example of how this might look in a large multi-organizational DLT implementation.

CERTIFICATE REVOCATION LISTS

When issuing certificates, it will occasionally be necessary to revoke those certificates before they naturally expire. We saw in the section on digital certificates how we can build expiry into the certificate, but if for example the credentials are compromised or perhaps an organization leaves the blockchain consortium, then it would be necessary to revoke their access earlier. When this occurs, the issuing CA adds the certificate to a CRL.

If you wanted to check the validity of a certificate then you would not only need to validate the certificate, but you should also check with the CA that the relevant certificate is not on the CRL (fig 10.7).

It is also possible to revoke the certificates of an ICA. This would collapse the Chain of Trust associated with that ICA. This is shown in figure 10.8.

As we mentioned earlier, after certificates and certificate authorities, the other half of the equation of this trust relationship is provided by MSP who limit access to the ledger based on these certificates. If the certificates are used to establish who an actor is in the system, the MSP defines what they are authorized to do.

MEMBERSHIP SERVICE PROVIDERS (MSPS)

In permissionless blockchains, it is enough to simply know who an actor is on the network. With a public and private key, we can establish the identity of any given person or account. With their private key, they can create signatures, generate transactions and sign them. With permissioned blockchains, we need to be able to exercise a greater amount of control over who is allowed to view information stored in the ledger, create certificates, administer the peers and create blocks and their content.

Once a CA has produced a certificate containing a public key which is coupled to a private key that is owned by the actor, the MSP's job is to provide approval against those public keys for given roles on the network. Putting this together with what we have already learned about blockchain

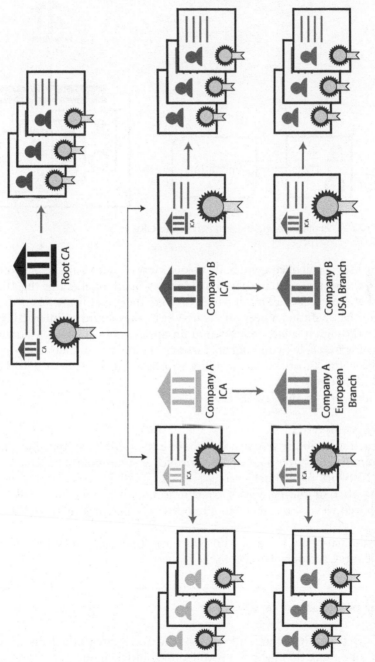

Figure 10.6 Multiple CAs and Intermediate CAs.

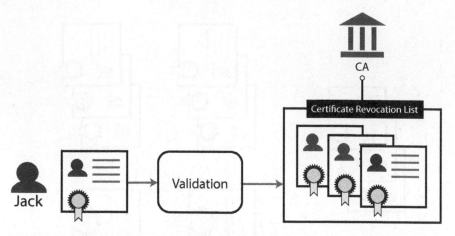

Figure 10.7 A certificate being checked against the CRL.

networks, we will once again build up our view of permissioned blockchains. So far, the system we have developed looks something like this (fig 10.9).

Sometimes those actors, having received their certificate from the CA, will not be operating a peer on the network, they could be interacting with a peer through a smart contract and an application. Imagine a distributed ledger for managing components for manufacturing. An actor may submit a request for an order. Their ability to order on the system will then be checked by the MSP.

MSPs work on two levels:

- Local-level
  Each node in the system would have a local MSP, establishing who has admin rights over a given peer or execute smart contracts, etc.
- Network or channel level
  As part of the network's configuration, all participants will have a shared view of membership, provided by a network-level MSP.

In summary, the CA and MSP work together using a system of digital certification, to control access to the ledger.

Key points about certification

- Determining who is allowed to read and write to the ledger is the one thing that defines a permissioned blockchain.
- It does this using Public Key Infrastructure or PKI.

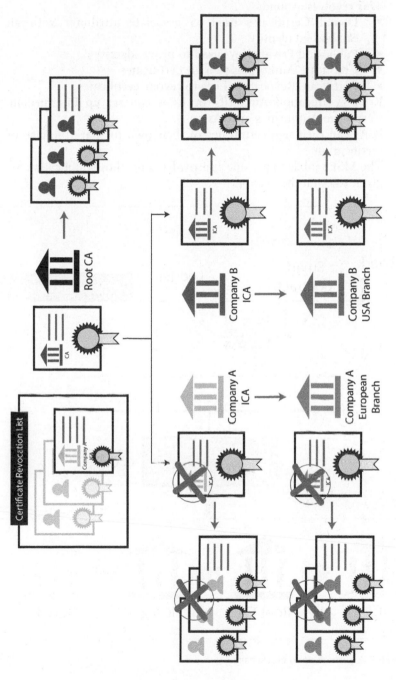

Figure 10.8 The Chain of Trust.

- This revolves around:
  - Digital Certificates used to associate attributes with an established identity
  - Public and Private Keys used to prove identity
  - Certificate Authorities to issue certificates
  - Certificate Revocation Lists to revoke certificates.
- Root Certification Authority or RCA can set up Intermediate Certificate Authorities or ICAs.
- ICAs can then sign certificates of their own to share the task of certification.
- The MSP's job is to provide approval against those public keys for given roles on the network.

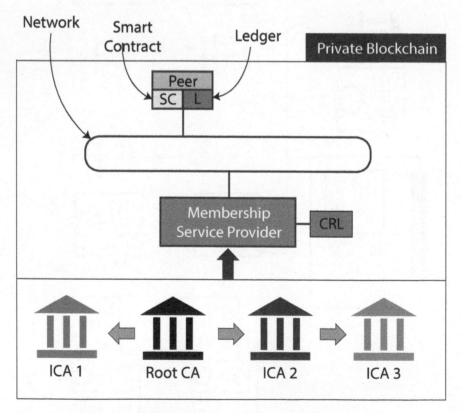

Figure 10.9 A permissioned blockchain.

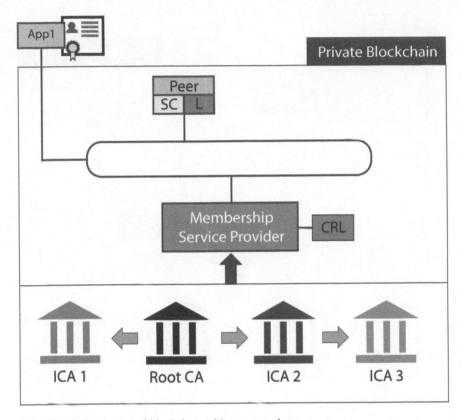

Figure 10.10 Permissioned blockchain with connected app.

ORDERING SERVICES

In permissionless blockchains, we have miners creating blocks and other nodes on the network checking their work. A consensus is formed on the blockchain over time, with any forks that appear being resolved as further blocks are mined. If I were to try and double-spend the funds that I had, only the first of the transactions to be accepted into the blockchain would be accepted. If a fork occurred where each of the two branches contained one of the two attempts to spend those funds, it would resolve and the second transaction would be rejected. In permissioned blockchains, this works slightly differently. Not only are we potentially working with transactions that are more complex than just inputs and outputs of UTXOs, but it is also often important in which order things happen. We do not need to and would not want to allow forks to occur and wait to see what order transactions occurred. For this reason, we use an ordering node or a collection of ordering nodes called an ordering service.

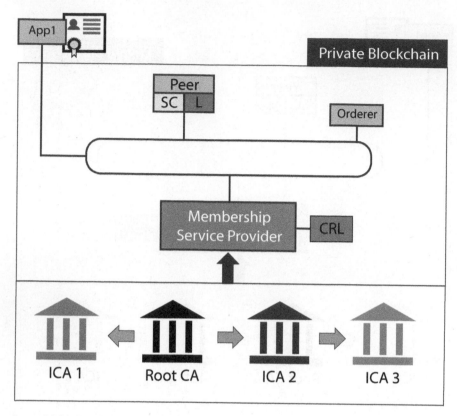

Figure 10.11 Permissioned blockchain with orderer.

This separation of ordering, from the peers which perform the actions of the smart contracts, allows for permissioned blockchains to be more scalable and efficient in ordering and execution when compared to permissionless blockchains.

CHANNELS

Sometimes an organization may not want other organizations to have access to certain content on their ledger. Perhaps our car manufacturer is in a consortium with suppliers of rubber for tyres, steel for panels and other component suppliers. They have a few applications associated with their system that allow them and their suppliers to interact with the smart contract.

The car manufacturer is a member of blockchain networks for two different suppliers. Each of the two supply chain DLTs could have other members on their channel but, to keep the diagram simple, we shall assume that they do not.

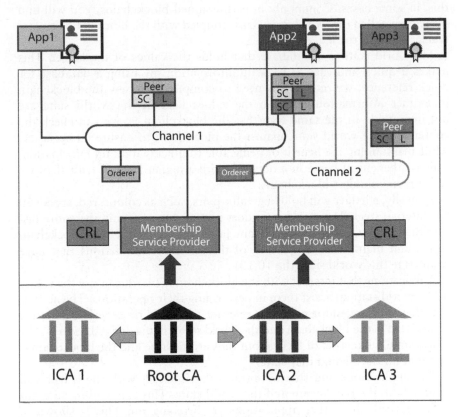

Figure 10.12 Permissioned blockchain with multiple channels.

Each channel is like a separate distributed ledger network of its own. Any given peer on the network could be a member of channel 1, channel 2 or both channels. In this situation, it is also possible that car manufacturer 1 was not aware of the separate channel with car manufacturer 2. As the two systems are only connected through their peers, there is nothing to let them know about each other. Each channel can have its own ledger, network configuration, including network-level MSP and its own certificate authorities.

In the diagram, we can see two channels in the network, where the car manufacturer is a member of both of the channels and the two component suppliers of steel and rubber are both a member of just one channel.

WORLD STATE

Though we have been using the term ledger as somewhat interchangeable with blockchain in this context up until now, there is a little more to it than this, in some cases. Commonly in permissioned blockchains, you will find something called the *world state*. This, coupled with the blockchain, is what is referred to as the ledger.

The world state is a database that holds the values of the ledger. This makes it quick and easy to look up information. By using a database for quick reference, we remove the need to completely review the blockchain to extract information. Though the values held in the world state are not immutable in the same way that the blockchain is, we can check the contents of the world state against the blockchain to ensure its accuracy, while maintaining the benefit of being able to quickly look up information. This is a benefit of being in a network with a higher level of trust than we see in permissionless blockchains.

Typically, a ledger will hold key-value pairs, such as colour: red, speed: 50 or material: steel. The world state does not need to maintain the entire history that is included in the blockchain, just the current state. The blockchain stores and maintains a log of all of the different transactions that have resulted in this world state (fig 10.13).

Applications that interact with the blockchain network can use the values in the world state to assist them in performing their operations. The actions that they take are endorsed by the relevant peers and those values can then be updated in the blockchain and the world state that is derived from it. The world state is like a set of facts about the current state and the blockchain is like that history behind that state.

The applications and smart contracts that interact with the ledger will update both the blockchain and the world state. This can lead to an event being flagged, that other applications are listening for. This is shown in figure 10.14.

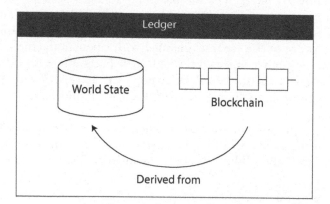

Figure 10.13 World state.

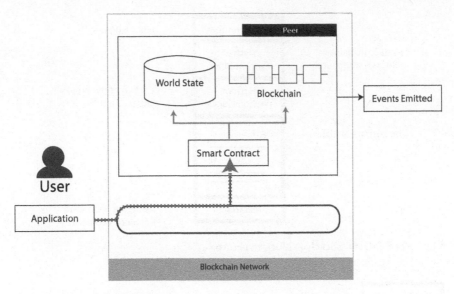

Figure 10.14 Data flow and events.

BLOCKS AND TRANSACTIONS

As permissioned blockchains are used for a variety of purposes, the most common are configurable in terms of their data structures and various other aspects. You will likely find the block and transactions structures quite familiar. The block structure of Hyperledger Fabric is shown in figure 10.15.

Block header structure from the Hyperledger documentation

There should be nothing surprising in these diagrams and will have come across all of them before, with the possible exception of the metadata section. If you do not recall any of the other items, look back to the section on block structure earlier in the book. The metadata section contains information about the block, such as the certification signature of its creator.

Transactions

Transaction structures are similar to those in permissioned blockchains, but rather than adopting either a UTXO or account model, they use proposals, responses and endorsements.

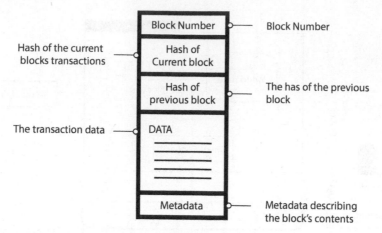

Figure 10.15 Private blockchain block structure.

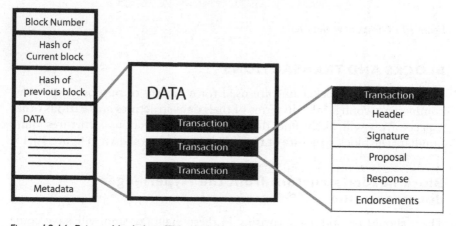

Figure 10.16 Private blockchain TX structure.

Transaction structure of Hyperledger Fabric, as described in the online documentation (Hyperledger 2020):

- Header
  This section contains metadata about the transaction. This could include information about the application and chain code that created it.
- Signature
  This section contains the signature of the transaction creator. It is needed to authenticate the transaction, in a permissioned environment.

- Proposal
  The proposal contains the proposed modifications to be enacted to the world state and added to the blockchain.
- Response
  This section shows the before and after values of the result of the actions being proposed.
- Endorsements
  These are endorsements of the transaction by its peers in the form of signatures on the response. The endorsers need to satisfy the requirement of the endorsement policy, which can be set to suit the requirement of the system. Normally each of the individual organizations in the consortium will sign off on transactions relevant to them.

CONSENSUS MECHANISMS

Given what we have already learned about consensus mechanisms, let us consider how they apply in permissioned contexts. Let's look at the two most common in permissionless blockchains:

- Proof of Work: In permissionless blockchains, PoW is currently king. The energy consumption, however, of trying to guess at valid hashes, is high and in a setting where we anticipate a lower level of malicious activity, it is arguably unnecessary.
- Proof of Stake: PoS and its variants are not practicable in most permissioned settings as they do not revolve around the use of a cryptocurrency. This makes staking that currency somewhat difficult. That is not to say that it could not be made to work, but it represents a less desirable option.

So what consensus mechanisms are most common in permissioned blockchains? That would be Practical Byzantine Fault Tolerance and Proof of Elapsed Time, used in Hyperledger's Fabric and Sawtooth implementations respectively. The lower computational cost and a higher degree of trust amongst peers make them more suitable choices.

Key points about permissioned blockchains

- Permissioned blockchains restrict access to the blockchain.
- Access controlled by Certification and Membership Service Providers.
- Ordering nodes take the transactions and place them into blocks.

- Each network can have several channels which are like blockchain networks in their own right.
- The contents of the blockchain are summarized in a World State Database for quick access.
- There is no need to use Proof of Work as there is a higher level of trust, so less resource-intensive consensus algorithms are more common.

REFERENCES

Creative Commons (2013) *Attribution 4.0 International.* Available at https://creativecommons.org/licenses/by/4.0/legalcode [Accessed 29 July 2021].

Hyperledger (2020) *Hyperledger Fabric – A blockchain Platform for the Enterprise.* Available at https://hyperledger-fabric.readthedocs.io/en/release-2.2/ [Accessed 28 July 2021].

Chapter 11

Privacy coins

When the first cryptocurrency arrived, it offered pseudo-anonymous management of currency. Although it is often thought of as being anonymous, since, at least in principle, you do not need to associate your name with your address, it is quite possible in some circumstances to deduce who an account belongs to as well as what they are doing with the funds they receive. The openness of the blockchain, for all to explore, allows a high degree of tracking and tracing to occur.

WHY IS PRIVACY IMPORTANT?

So why might this be a bad thing? Well, people generally feel it is an invasion of their privacy to share their financial records with the world. Besides this, it can leave people open to real-world or online attacks, if they are known to be high-net-worth individuals. They could be targeted for a robbery or hacking. They may also wish to avoid having government agencies look through all of their personal records.

For these reasons, attempts have been made to increase the privacy provided by cryptocurrencies. We have already looked at coin mixing in a previous section, which attempts to obscure the sending and receiving of coins, by mixing them with others. In this section, we will look at various other attempts to increase the privacy provided to users of cryptocurrencies.

Before we look at the steps taken though, let us understand the key issues with regards to privacy at the moment. These are *Know Your Customer* (KYC) legislation and *on-chain analysis*.

KYC LEGISLATION

The Financial Task Force or FATF is an intergovernmental organization that develops policy to protect the global financial systems. It has created strict standards on crypto assets in 2020 which many third party crypto-companies are adhering to. As the name suggests, KYC requires companies to know who their customers are, typically by holding details in the form of

DOI: 10.1201/9781003187165-11

their name, country, address, data-of-birth and so on as well as verification of this by passports, ID cards, driving licenses, and so on.

One of the key issues that this legislation is supposed to tackle is money laundering. The EU has issued Anti Money Laundering Directive 5 (AMLD5) with similar effect. Both of these result in more KYC as the laws outlaw anonymity on currency transfers.

ON-CHAIN ANALYSIS

This is essentially looking at the blockchains of the various cryptocurrencies and attempting to link transactions. We have already had a look at blocks on both Bitcoin and Ethereum blockchains and seen how it is possible to look and see transaction values, as well as its inputs and output.

Imagine that you send Bitcoin to someone. You could look on the blockchain using a block explorer and search for the address that was provided to see other funds they have received. Originally Satoshi thought that people could use new key pairs for each transaction. This was not always done in practice though and many wallets will not offer this option.

Another problem with this appears when you need to use multiple inputs to create a transaction. When you see a transaction with multiple inputs, it is a reasonably safe assumption that the two addresses are linked to one owner. In this way, it is possible to start linking accounts and their transactions together.

Figure 11.1 shows four transactions.

Transaction 1 is from an unknown person to someone that we have previously identified as Jill. This could have been through KYC or another less direct method. Transactions 2 and 3 are between unknown parties and transaction 4 is from two of those unknown parties (solid-dark filled and diagonal-stripe filled) to another unknown party with some change sent back to the diagonal-stripes account. Now we could already tell something from what we have seen here already, but let's see what happens next (fig 11.2).

Because the large majority of transactions with multiple inputs come from one wallet combining UTXOs from different accounts, we can conclude with enough confidence that the solid-dark-colour account is also owned by Jill. As the solid-dark account has also been used in combined inputs with the solid-light account, we can also deduce that the solid-light account is owned by Jill.

The linking of transactions to accounts and those accounts to people can be done by individuals, or it can be done by organizations. One such company who specialize in this are Chainalysis, whose services are reportedly used by the FBI, IRS, law enforcement, DEA, CIA, as well as similar in different countries including Europol and national police in the UK.

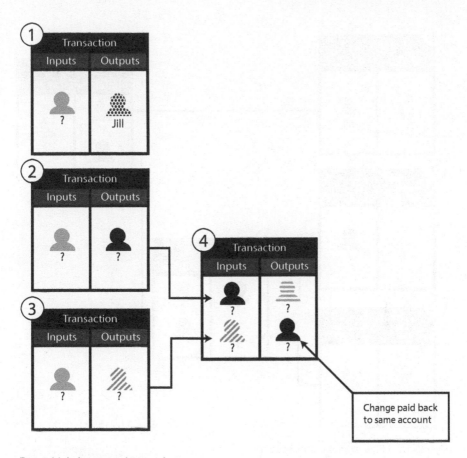

Figure 11.1 An example set of transactions.

Chainalysis allow their clients to track "bad actors" who attract their attention by being associated in some way with

- Stolen funds from hacking
- Terrorist financing
- Ransomware payout addresses
- People who use mixers
- Darknet marketplaces.

They use the data that they find on the blockchain together with other information such as IP address, to attempt to associate accounts to people and determine who is sending money and to whom.

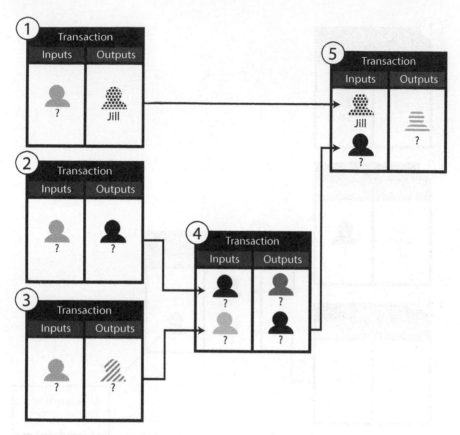

Figure 11.2 More example transactions.

ANONYMITY SET

When reviewing on-chain data with the intention of identifying who a particular transaction has been sent to, one key question is "How large is the anonymity set?" This question is asking "How many people could be the receiver of a transaction?" Let's look at the mixing example we used earlier. This time the names are blanked out, except for our account of interest, which is labelled AoI and shown in a darker shade (fig 11.3).

We had several people sending money to a wallet used for mixing and this shows the inputs to the wallet. The coins are later sent onto other wallets, which is shown in the figure 11.4.

We want to identify which account received the money from our account of interest. So, our anonymity set is the number of people who received coins from the wallet (fig 11.5).

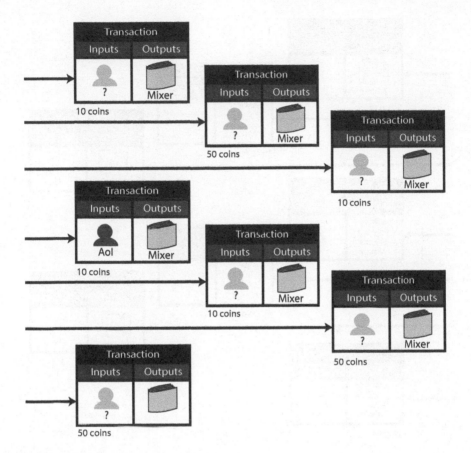

Figure 11.3 **Example coins sent to mixer.**

We can use some basic deduction to narrow this though. The senders added in different values, so we can reduce this set to include only those with a suitable amount (fig 11.6).

There is also a delay period between the coins being sent to the mixer and the mixer delivering the coins to the recipient wallet. The anonymity set should not include everyone who has ever sent funds to the wallet, instead it should be limited only to those who send it within a particular period, in which the mixer sends those transactions. This reduces the anonymity set yet further (fig 11.7).

Besides limitations of the anonymity set, another criticism of the mixing method is that it requires a third party service. This means that you have to trust the third party not to steal or lose your funds. They are completely

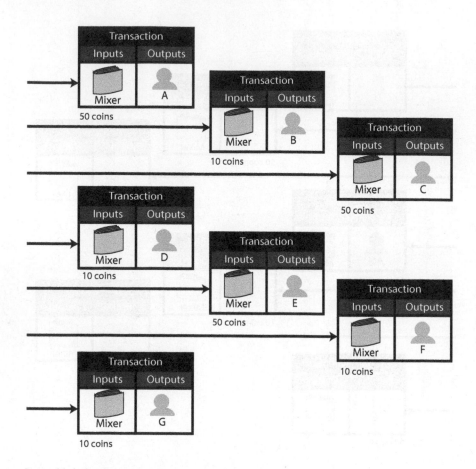

Figure 11.4 Coins sent from mixer to wallets.

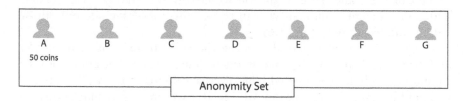

Figure 11.5 Anonymity set of the mixer.

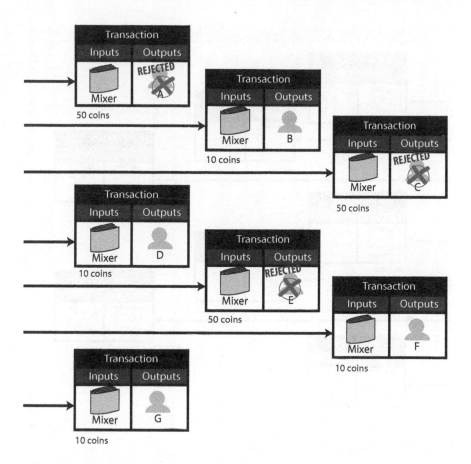

Figure 11.6 Anonymity set reduced by amount.

out of your control once you have transferred them and so you are a trust relationship with a centralized service.

HD WALLETS

In a modification of Satoshi's planned approach to Bitcoin wallets, Hierarchical Deterministic wallets or HD wallets add an index to the Bitcoin address to determine new wallet addresses – this could be customer ID or some other integer value.

Remembering what we learned about Elliptic Curve Cryptography, the private key is the number of transformations and the public key is the point on the curve. We can add the number to the private key and add the number

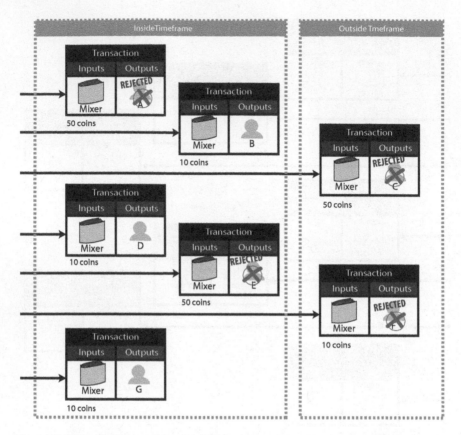

Figure 11.7 Anonymity set reduced by time.

of transformations to the public key and this allows the sender to easily generate new addresses with the shared key. The receiver can provide the sender with an address based on this shared key and use the modified private key to sign for transactions when they come to spend it.

The wallet then contains several values, with several different private/public key combinations.

An example

Private key = 43   (normally the number would be many times greater)
Public key = 43 *P*   (this is a coordinate on the Elliptic curve)
Shared secret = 12   (this could be an invoice number or other number known to both parties)

New Private key = 55   (this is the key that will unlock the transaction)
New Public key = 55 P (this is the key that the funds should be sent to)

Note: Satoshi (2008) said:

a new key pair should be used for each transaction to keep them from being linked to a common owner. Some linking is still unavoidable with multi-input transactions, which necessarily reveal that their inputs were owned by the same owner. The risk is that if the owner of a key is revealed, linking could reveal other transactions that belonged to the same owner.

COINJOIN

This technique was suggested in an attempt to resolve the associating of accounts by allowing unrelated people to join their transactions into one single transaction with multiple inputs and outputs. This is important because it means that one cannot rely on the association of input accounts to be the same person. This complicates chain analysis. This is a very similar approach to coin mixing. Both these techniques have the benefit that they do not require any changes to the fundamental functionality and code of the cryptocurrency (fig 11.8).

DASH COIN

Dash coin uses what it calls PrivateSend which extends the UTXO model with a form of CoinJoin. Dash allows its users to have additional wallet addresses which they can load with private funds by declaring that they want to transfer an amount to that address. A master node takes inputs from them and at least two other people transferring similar amounts and mixes them to a new address under your control.

To further separate inputs from their owners this happens in rounds of different denominations (0.001, 0.01, 0.1, 1 and 10 dash). The funds in the new wallet address are then ready to spend. This has the advantage of being able to have more private coins ready to spend quickly.

The disadvantages are that the master nodes still need to know who is sending what to whom. This makes it vulnerable to both hacking and interested entities running a master node to track payments. Additionally, it is also clear to others that you have used the CoinJoin method, implemented

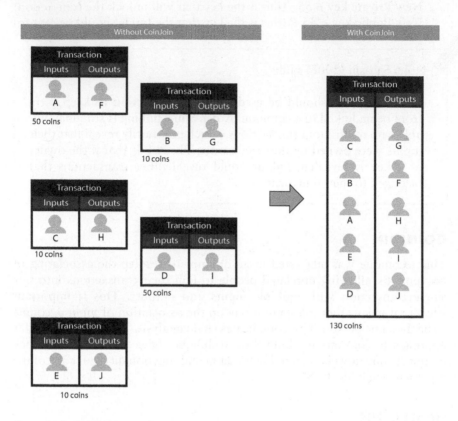

Figure 11.8 CoinJoin example.

to try and obscure transactions which can itself highlight your account to those who might want to take a closer look.

MONERO AND CRYPTONOTE

Arguably the most private of coins available is Monero. There are other coins available that work on the same principle, however, with features introduced with CryptoNote. Monero is probably the best known and most widely used of these.

With this cryptocurrency, a range of new concepts was introduced to limit on-chain analysis of transaction data. These obscure the

- Sender address
- Recipient address
- And the quantity sent.

This is done through the use of three new concepts: stealth addresses, ring signatures and confidential transactions. These are known as RingCT. Let's explore how they work.

STEALTH ADDRESSES

When we looked at HD wallets, we learned that a shared secret can be added to a wallet's public and private keys, to adjust the address, so that we have a new address for each transaction. Stealth addresses do something similar, but the shared secret, rather than having to be agreed beforehand, is a very large, randomly generated secret number that is added to the address. This number is then included in the transaction data. To stop anyone from being able to read the shared secret and work out the root address, it is encoded with the receiver's public key.

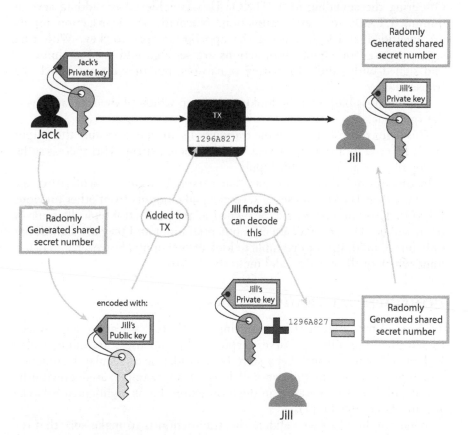

Figure 11.9 Stealth address example.

This means that, rather than scanning the blockchain for UTXOs associated with your public key as you would with other cryptocurrencies, you are instead scanning the blockchain for UTXOs that have addresses that your key can decrypt. When you find it, you can add that shared key to your private key and derive the address for that individual transaction.

This results in every transaction on the Monero blockchain having to use an individual address. This creates a virtually infinite anonymity set. When the addresses are unique every time, it could have been sent to anyone.

It does, however, mean that when Jack sends coins to Jill, he can watch the blockchain and see when Jill has spent them. This limits Jill's privacy and that is where *ring signature* come in.

RING SIGNATURES

Ring signatures are implemented in privacy coins with the intention of obscuring the spending of a UTXO. This is achieved by adding several dummy UTXOs to every transaction. Normally the transaction inputs are identified and signed using the appropriate private key. With ring signatures, several similar transactions are selected and used as dummies and signed with validly formatted signatures, but they do not match the transaction.

It is not possible to tell by looking at them, which of the transactions is the valid one.

This helps to obscure when the transactions are spent because the output could be used in a dummy TX or could be being spent. This increases the anonymity set of the possible inputs.

In this example, let us imagine that person D wants to send 10 coins. They use their UTXO and select several equal amounts from other previous UTXOs. These do not need to be owned by person D and typically none of them will be. They provide them as potential input and they are signed, but only one is valid. It is not possible to look at the inputs, however, and determine which of them is the valid input (fig 11.10).

CONFIDENTIAL TRANSACTIONS

To conceal the amounts that are being transferred, we are going to need to return to our Elliptic Curve Cryptography and use a technique called Pederson Commitments. Let's start by considering a regular transaction and its values. To do this we will look at an example used previously. Specifically, we are interested in the transaction that is highlighted between Joe and James (fig 11.11).

What we do when we validate this transaction is to make sure that the outputs equal the inputs, so $18 + 5 = 23$. We have two inputs, which we will

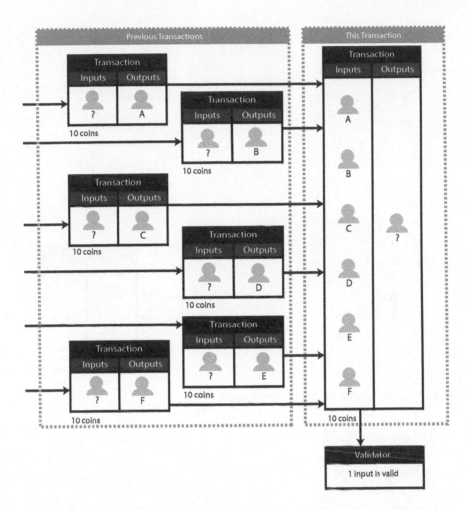

Figure 11.10 Ring signatures example.

label A and B, and one output, which we will label C. So, what we can say is we are happy so long as

$$A+B=C$$

We can do this same thing using points on an elliptic curve, just like we did in the previous section. If we once again use P as our point, and our values are V_1, V_2 and V_3 it would look something like this:

$$V_1.P + V_2.P = V_3.P.$$

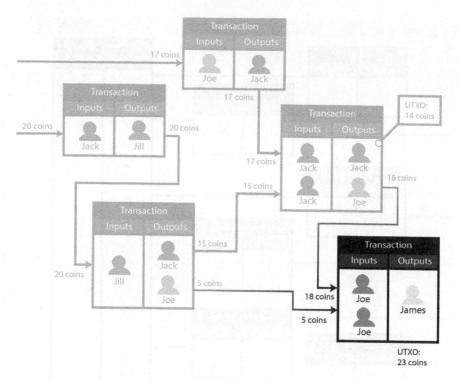

Figure 11.11 Example for confidential transactions.

So, to use our example from above:

$$18.P + 5.P = 23.P.$$

As the size of the values we will be using are comparatively small, or at least in computing where a few million mathematical operations are quite easy to calculate, it would be easy enough to work out what these values would be. To do this we would only have to start with point P and work out the following relatively small number of points and we could calculate what these values might be by brute force.

To prevent this, a randomly generated large number R and a new binding point G is added to each side, called a binding factor. These new values are such that

$$R_1 + R_2 = R_3.$$

Because of what we know about elliptic curve cryptography, we can therefore also know that:

$$R_1.G + R_2.G = R_3.G.$$

Though the actual values would be significantly larger and less uniform, a simple example of this would be:

$$5,000,000.R + 6,000,000.R = 11,000,000.R.$$

You can see how the above equation would take a longer time to process than the example above which uses much lower numbers. It does not, however, do anything for us like this as it is just two numbers adding together to equal another large number. To obscure our initial transaction then, we need to combine the two equations. When we add these to the equation, we get something like this:

$$\left(V_1.P + R_1.G\right) + \left(V_2.P + R_2.G\right) = \left(V_3.P + R_3.G\right).$$

Anything we add to both sides will still result in a balanced equation, and so it will still be valid. It will not, however, be possible to see from the outside what the transaction is worth.

Let's have a look at some real-life information from a Monero block and we can see some of the more private transactions on the blockchain.

Here you will see many properties that you will be familiar with from previous sections. One that you might be unfamiliar with is the Mixin property, set to 10. This value is the number of other transactions that are used as decoy transactions by the ring signature. You can see these in the following transaction information.

Transaction Hash: e45ce625b86b7b6b85a3ae6a3bd6a5011db9dba1955f6e6646fbabfadd36c5e3

1 Input		2 Outputs

Details

Confirmations	292162
Block	2123202
Difficulty	298097639554
Fee	0.000019060000 XMR
Mixin	10

Figure 11.12 A transaction summary from the Monero blockchain.

Number	Block	Public key
1	2071183	c2087211e71428b12d01683d81a5e83dd431e59637eb258941c061c23b5751c3
2	2083885	03a8fd19c027b37a2087b80a9d7323705592c53e0dc3c97c7d91f875497091bd
3	2112995	967776e11a6ce05bf3bdcc77760b5fc92554f21a5f7c053145a3cf5ccbab5fef
4	2114526	2132cc93a3eda36ecc06d15fba0311d735c202713696c29258d4bbb42f17d8c6
5	2122310	ed2381deb24bfcda090000427c27ea0fb657570a991527202ae0cd619981b359
6	2122753	0f2487f4fa6c5321a762b432ffe5b9f0a8a8f83e7784d741cd348b66ae1545b6
7	2122799	7e46d5ac1a7000835ae741fef643fd9c4dbab61fd0294353e074a00ce2115cd0
8	2122885	4e5fafae97821a6d51cd5acbcb1b27dfb457c23307450ffa3f4dfe4c780725da
9	2122892	a8a224ecce2fc5a3c780b3d17342f30c8faada31ee5f84fac8143 4a42fede404
10	2122905	4eb29b02e865a213a6014d4f302e18bc4a3f26b3615277b67fdc486bf0ee0ad0
11	2122906	e78b93b70330e68a4ff2b71c9e2e9b5e2c9f0f819cbaa9302935d179b3220200

Figure 11.13 Transaction inputs of a Monero transaction.

Number	Public key
1	eb6b57e58af108fc3cfcd3c0a3f06419275a88ae29921c52c97e468e9379dc85
2	608e2084197980ce3345aeefba18696f8677bc023f5ccf4b56822de0b280d293

Figure 11.14 Transaction outputs from a Monero transaction.

Note all of the decoy transactions. Each of them appears valid, however many are decoys.

Some coins have always-on privacy like Monero, others like Dash do not, and only have the capacity to be more private. Even when using the privacy function on a coin like Dash, the Monero-style coins are more private as including all transactions in the privacy set increases the anonymity set.

Monero is a very private coin. For this reason, it falls foul of many exchanges KYC policies. The exchanges cannot track or trace the coins and anti-money laundering regulations may leave them vulnerable to claims that they are facilitating money laundering, dark web purchases or other nefarious activity. This had led to some exchanges refusing to trade in Monero out of fear of the legal repercussions.

There are some things that you can do that will not draw attention from authorities by mixing or be limited by restrictions on coins that cannot be easily purchased. They include:

- Using an HD wallet and taking care to use new addresses each time.
- Use a VPN to reduce the likelihood of having your IP associated with your real-world identity.

FLOODING, GOSSIP PROTOCOL AND TX TRANSMISSION

As we have seen in previous chapters, particularly the section on mempools, when a transaction enters a network it is sent on to other nodes and they send it onto yet further nodes in a process known as flooding or gossip protocol.

If you control a significant number of nodes on a network, it is possible, through determining when the transaction reached each of your nodes, to determine the likely location of the node that generated it.

Consider this example where I control the darker nodes. A TX is added to the mempool and flooding begins from the TX labelled point (fig 11.15).

The nodes that are connected to the origin point then receive the transaction and add it their mempool (fig 11.16).

who then pass it to the nodes that they are connected to (fig 11.17).

Eventually the transaction floods across the network. You can see, by listening for the time that the transaction arrives, it is possible to draw conclusions about where it originated.

Understanding that the transmission times are likely to be shorter when the nodes are closer to each other, if I wanted to hone-in on a particular address, I could spin up a number of nodes across the world and determine which nodes received the transactions generated by that address first. Then I could localize a group of nodes around that location, and do the same again, to localize the origin of the transaction.

To help protect against this, the broadcasting of transactions to nodes can take place on a randomized timer. This helps provide some protection, but this is not flawless.

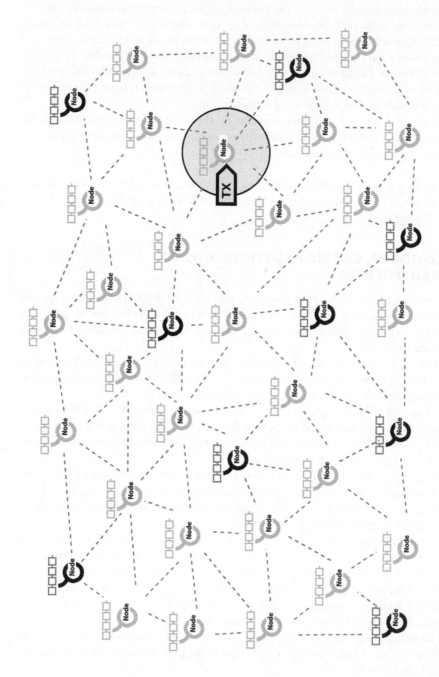

Figure 11.15 Flooding start point.

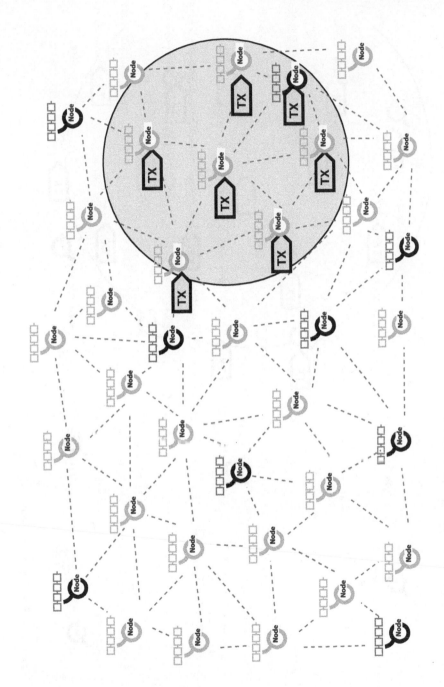

Figure 11.16 Flooding to immediately connected nodes.

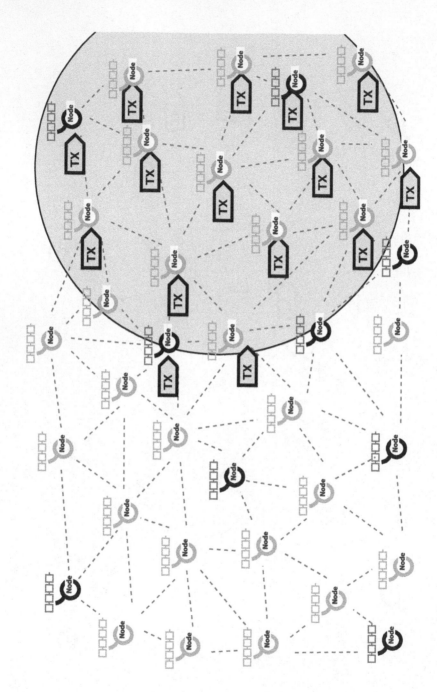

Figure 11.17 Flooding to next nodes.

IP ADDRESSES

It is possible to link people to IP addresses. When you add transactions to the mempool, though the IP address is not added to the transaction data, it is possible to see who created the transaction by the monitoring of IP addresses and the monitoring of where and how the transaction spreads across the network. This is not desirable for those who wish to remain anonymous and have their transactions be private.

DANDELION

The dandelion protocol is a solution to this. Though there are variations and improvements on this, the concept is essentially a modification of the same approach. In this approach, there are two phases, a stem phase and a fluff phase.

- Stem phase/anonymity phase: In this phase, the initial transaction is received. Rather than propagating it directly around the network, it is passed on to only one randomly selected peer. They then pass it onto another randomly selected peer. This happens several times until randomly it enters the fluff phase.
- The fluff phase/spreading phase: In this phase, the transaction begins to propagate around the network by diffusion, in much the same way that it would have before. Because of the actions taken in the stem phase, however, it is no longer possible to determine the origin of the transaction by monitoring the time of arrival across the network.

In figure 11.18 you can see how the identity of the transaction creator is obscured by changing the point of origin. It is also quite clear to see how the dandelion protocol got its name! You can see from the above that, even with a large network of peers under my control, I cannot determine the origin point. If I receive the TX in the stem phase, I will not know how many peers had received it before me and the fluff phase no longer helps to determine the origin.

Key points about privacy and privacy coins

- Privacy is important as it allows users to protect themselves.
- Know Your Customer legislation seeks to ensure businesses can identify their customers.
- On-Chain Analysis is used to associate blockchain addresses to real-world identities.

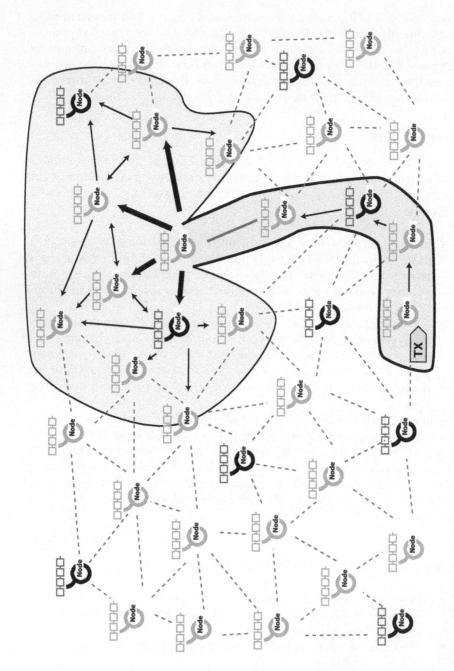

Figure 11.18 Dandelion path.

- An anonymity set it the number of possible identities that a given address can be narrowed down to.
- HD Wallets automate the production of several Public/Private Key combinations associated with the same individual or organization.
- CoinJoin attempts to resolve the associating of accounts by joining multiple transactions into one, with multiple inputs and outputs.
- Stealth addresses are used to hide recipient, by adding a shared secret to the receiver's address and then encrypting this with the receiver's public key.
- Ring signatures obscure the sender by adding several dummy UTXOs to every transaction.
- Confidential transactions use ECC theory and Pederson Commitments to obscure the amount being transacted.
- Dandelion Protocol is used distribute the transaction across the network before flooding to obscure its origin point.

REFERENCE

Nakamoto, S. (2008) *Bitcoin: A Peer-to-Peer Electronic Cash System* Available at https://nakamotoinstitute.org/Bitcoin/ [Accessed 29 July 2021].

Chapter 12

Blockchains and cryptocurrency issues and answers

ADOPTION

Another issue is the level of adoption. Being a new technology, relatively speaking, it has a lower level of adoption when compared to other mechanisms for storing and transferring wealth. All forms of wealth are dependent on unspoken agreement on the value of the asset, which is created from scarcity and the supply and demand that creates this. Just like any other asset, it derives its value from its use. Unless a critical mass of adopters is reached it cannot reach its potential.

There are many attempts to engage the public and corporations with crypto-assets. Companies such as crypto.com and Wirex are working to integrate cryptocurrencies with traditional payment mechanisms, using credit cards and gift vouchers. A new starter Tari is working to add privacy and trading to Digital Rights Management (DRM) assets to get large holders of DRM such as Cinematic and music studios onboard and pushing privacy tokens specifically to increase adoption.

SCALING

As we have seen, the number of transactions it is possible to process in a given period is limited by the block size and the speed with which a block is created. It is not feasible to decrease the time between blocks, as this is required to prevent forking. Increasing block size, despite being advocated by some, is also not without complication.

Larger blocks require more storage space. This is unavoidable if the blockchain is to contain more transactions, regardless of how they are held. By increasing the block size, however, we are increasing the amount that has to be distributed in one go when a block is added. A 10 mb block would take longer to flood through the network than a 1 mb block, for example. From what we have learned already about forking and block time, we can see that this will have implications for forking too.

DOI: 10.1201/9781003187165-12

There is no single solution to the scaling problem that is universally accepted. Some advocate for larger block sizes, others argue that this only serves to delay the issue and a different solution needs to be found. Disagreement on the matter has led to some hard forks of Bitcoin including Bitcoin Cash, Bitcoin XT, Bitcoin Classic and Bitcoin Unlimited which adapted the Bitcoin protocol to support an increase to the maximum block size.

Another aspect of the same issue is the speed at which transactions take place. When fewer transactions can be processed in each block, it takes longer to process transactions. This will, of course, have further implications for the cost of the transactions.

Possible solutions to these issues can be provided by what is known as Layer Two solutions.

LAYER TWO SOLUTIONS

If we consider the blockchain and all its constituent parts that we have discussed so far as being Layer One, then Layer Two solutions are systems built on top of this. They are not part of the blockchain, but they can provide tools and services to interact with it, in a manner that enhances their capability. Primarily they do this by moving some of the computation off-chain. As we have seen, computation on the blockchain must be done by every node on the system. This makes it computationally expensive to perform tasks on the blockchain. Because they are based on the blockchain, this acts as a trustless anchor for the system and is the ultimate arbiter of truth.

The Lightning Network is probably the best-known Layer Two technology and we will look at this network and use it as an example of why you might want to do this and what can be achieved.

LIGHTNING NETWORK

The Lightning Network is a payment protocol which allows for near-instantaneous transactions. It does this by avoiding the requirement to add transactions to a block and await several confirmations before the transactions are confirmed.

With this method, a channel is set up between the parties that wish to transact. Imagine Jack frequents Jill's coffee shop with some regularity. He wishes to be able to make quick transactions in a cryptocurrency to pay for the coffee and Jill also wishes to accept this cryptocurrency in exchange for her coffee. They establish a channel, which is a separate ledger between them. In this instance, the currency is flowing in one direction, from Jack to Jill, so Jack funds the initial channel. At this point, the funds that he uses are locked into the channel in the same way that smart contracts can lock in funds. The transaction for this is added to the blockchain.

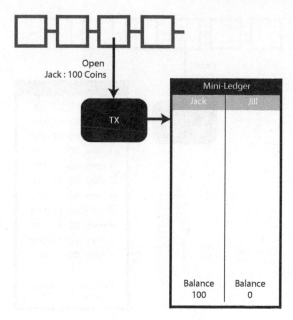

Figure 12.1 Lightning Network opening.

Now each time that Jack buys a coffee that costs one coin, that transaction is added to this channel's ledger, rather than going onto the blockchain (fig 12.2).

Only when the channel is closed is another transaction added to the blockchain, which resolves the balance of the separate ledger (fig 12.3).

In this example the currency was flowing in only one direction; however the channel could be set up with funds from both parties with transactions going in both directions, for example where people are trading back and forth.

The benefit of transacting in this manner is that it is possible to take those computations off-chain so that they happen quickly. It also saves in the amount that one pays to create a transaction, as rather than 10 transactions being added to the blockchain that would happen in the above coffee example, there are only transactions to open and close the channel.

By setting up these channels, which are mini-ledgers, with smaller numbers of transactions on the blockchain, we are speeding up the process and reducing the load on Layer One. This helps to make blockchain payments more scalable and makes microtransactions more feasible.

Much like everything else, the Lightning Network is not without criticism. There are arguments about the extent of its usefulness. After all, it is not useful for one-off transactions, as to create a channel and then use it once would replace one transaction with two. That is unless the micro-ledger is

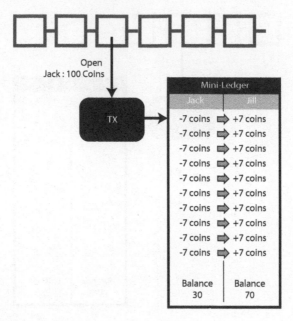

Figure 12.2 Lightning Network in use.

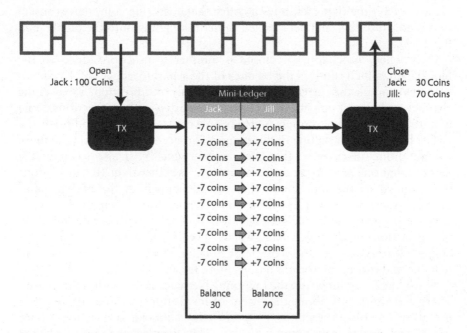

Figure 12.3 Lightning Network closing.

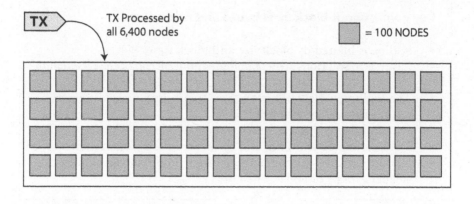

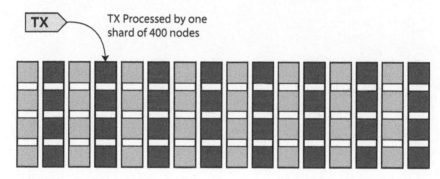

Figure 12.4 Sharding example.

managed across a range of services in a centralized manner and we have
discussed many reasons why centralization is avoided in previous sections.

Another solution, to the limitations above, is that of sharding, which is a
Layer One technology, rather than the Layer Two approach of the Lightning
Network.

SHARDING

The concept behind sharding is relatively straight forward. To process more
transactions, rather than having all nodes working to create and verify
the next block and its transactions, the network of nodes is divided into
sub-groups, known as shards. Each shard can then process transactions in
parallel.

One consideration around sharding is that it takes fewer nodes to assume
control of a shard than it does to assume control over the entire network of
nodes. We will look at this in a little more detail in the coming section on
attacks.

Key points about blockchain issues and resolutions

- Scaling is limited by block size and block time.
- Layer Two solutions are technologies built on top of the blockchain network.
- The Lightning Network is a Layer Two solution that attempts to resolve the scaling problem.
- It establishes a mini-ledger between two parties where smaller amounts can be sent back and forth until the contract is closed.
- Sharding divides the computation done on the blockchain among smaller groups of nodes, or shards.

Chapter 13

Attacks

The majority of attacks on cryptocurrencies are not the types of attacks that are specific to cryptocurrencies. They tend to be attacks that are used on various computer systems, such as hacking and phishing. There are however some considerations that are particular to cryptocurrency and it is these that we will discuss below.

PRIVATE KEY/WALLET ATTACK

A cryptocurrency wallet has to have a copy of the private key to be able to sign transactions. This private key is probably the greatest point of vulnerability, in that if someone were to gain access to the private key, they would be able to sign transactions and spend the UTXOs/account balances. Typically, the private keys are protected by passwords, which is fairly effective, though there are plenty of examples of users either not paying adequate attention to the security of their private keys or seed phrases or being tricked into passing them on to others. Again, this is not so much an issue with cryptocurrencies any more than failing to secure the PIN for your bank card or giving it out is an issue with the banking system.

51 PER CENT ATTACK

This is perhaps the best known of the cryptocurrency attacks. It centres on the level of control that you have if you can control more than half of the hash power of the network of nodes. As we have seen in previous sections, with Proof of Work, the nodes with the most hash power have more control over what is written to the blockchain. This gives the person who controls those nodes certain possibilities that they would not otherwise have, such as double-spending.

Imagine that we have a situation in which I am controlling more than half of the nodes on the network. In actuality, I could just be controlling fewer nodes, so long as they produce more hashes that the other nodes. If I wanted

DOI: 10.1201/9781003187165-13

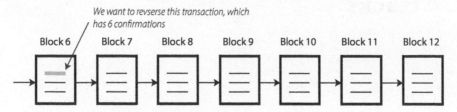

We want to revserse this transaction, which has 6 confirmations

| Block 6 | Block 7 | Block 8 | Block 9 | Block 10 | Block 11 | Block 12 |

Figure 13.1 A 51 per cent attack – target TX.

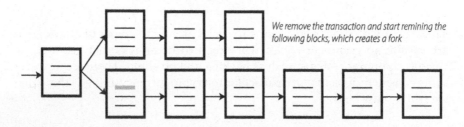

We remove the transaction and start remining the following blocks, which creates a fork

Figure 13.2 A 51 per cent attack – removing and remining blocks.

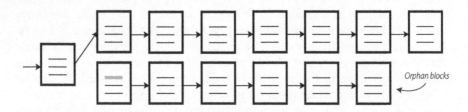

Orphan blocks

Figure 13.3 A 51 per cent attack – complete.

to reverse a transaction in block 6 then I would instruct my nodes to cut off the blocks from that point onwards, ignore updates from the "honest blockchain" and then I need to re-mine the following blocks.

As I hold more hash power than the other machines on the network, my chain will grow faster and as soon as it is longer, the other machines will accept it.

If I did not hold most of the hash power, this would be impossible as the other nodes blockchain would grow faster than mine and so they would never accept my fraudulent version of the blockchain. As I do, in this case, hold most of the hash power, I can keep mining blocks, while refusing to update with the "honest blockchain" until my version of the blockchain is longer. At this point, my version of the blockchain is accepted by everyone and I have effectively unspent that transaction.

There is still, however, a signed transaction for the UTXO in existence, so just to make sure that it cannot still be applied, I need to take those funds and transfer them to a different wallet, so that transaction is no longer valid.

Such an attack has already taken place in cryptocurrency, but only on networks with low hash rates. The larger the network, the more secure it is against these attacks. It would be very difficult to conduct such an attack against Bitcoin as it would take a massive investment to secure over half of the hash power, whereas smaller cryptocurrencies would require much less.

SELFISH MINING/SHADOW MINING

Selfish mining, sometimes known as shadow mining, is where you mine blocks but do not distribute them across the network and instead keep them to your nodes, to gain some advantage. Imagine that I have around 50 per cent of the hash power of the network and I discover a new block, rather than passing it around and letting other nodes work on this new blockchain, I keep it to my nodes (fig 13.4).

This effectively creates a fork in the blockchain where my nodes are working on the top branch and others are working on the lower branch (fig 13.5).

While the other systems are busy wasting energy looking for this block, I am busy mining the next one. After several blocks, I release the new blocks in one go. This shuts down the top branch and my version becomes the accepted chain, meaning I take all of the transaction fees and block reward for these blocks (fig 13.6).

I can then start the process again. This would mean that nearly all blocks would be mined by my nodes from this point onwards.

This also introduces the potential for double-spend. Imagine I am sending transactions to the nodes on the top branch and spending my UTXOs. While this is happening, I am making sure not to include those transactions in my blocks and instead include a transaction that transfers those same funds to a wallet under my control (fig 13.7).

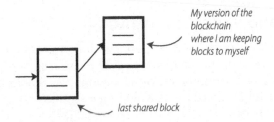

Figure 13.4 Selfish mining – beginning.

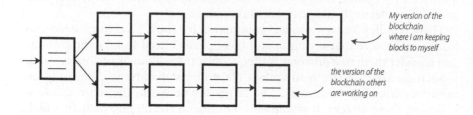

Figure 13.5 Selfish mining – in progress.

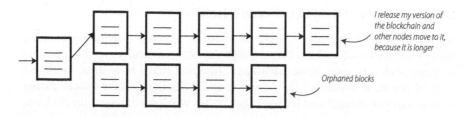

Figure 13.6 Selfish mining – complete.

When eventually my blocks are distributed across the network, they will effectively be reversing the spending of those transactions and the funds will be returned to my possession.

CENSORING TRANSACTIONS

In the same manner, by controlling the blocks added to the chain, I could, if I wanted to, block transactions from a particular address. All I would have to do is instruct my nodes not to accept these transactions or accept blocks with those transactions in and they would never make it into the accepted version of the blockchain. This is, of course, not what cryptocurrencies are supposed to achieve!

SINGLE-SHARD-TAKEOVER ATTACK

In previous sections, we have discussed sharding, the concept of dividing computation done on the blockchain into different shards. When considering the 51 per cent attack from the previous section, you should be able to see how this is affected by sharding. It would take significantly fewer nodes to control a single shard.

In much the same way as before, malicious nodes controlling one shard can modify transactions. To prevent this, we need to make sure that nodes

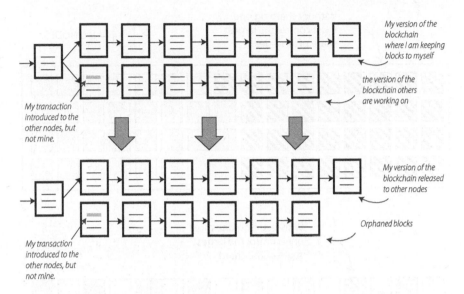

Figure 13.7 Selfish mining double-spend.

are allocated to shards in such a manner that grouping is avoided. Another preventative measure is to require endorsement by more than 50 per cent of the nodes in the shard (fig 13.8).

SYBIL ATTACK

A Sybil attack is any attack based on creating multiple identities. There are various examples of this in other non-blockchain areas, such as the pseudo-Sybil attack of "fake media" spread by bots. These multiple identities owned by the same person or organization are commonly referred to as sock-puppet accounts. In "fake media" sock-puppets are used to falsely increase engagement with stories so that they are disproportionately reflected in searches, to influence viewers.

In blockchains, Sybil attacks can be used for a variety of purposes. One such purpose is to control a particular node and its understanding of the blockchain. In this example, we surround a target node and control its view of the blockchain, by effectively disconnecting it from the other nodes.

Figure 13.9 shows the highlighted node surrounded and its view of the blockchain being determined by nodes under the attacker's control.

This could theoretically have implications for double-spending, where the surrounded node did not know that the UTXO had already been spent. Of course, if we are waiting for six confirmations, we are unlikely to be able

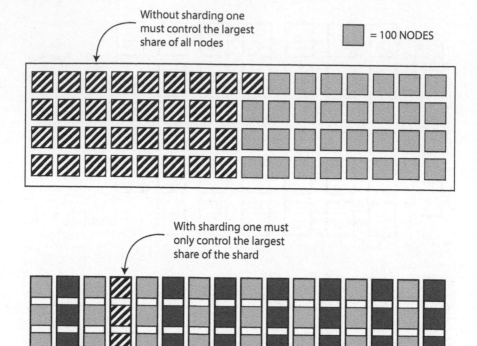

Figure 13.8 One per cent attack.

to provide these with a small number of nodes and so conducting such an attack becomes difficult in the extreme, but it is theoretically possible.

> Note: Sybil attacks are named after a character from a book called Sybil, who suffered from dissociative identity disorder.

A Sybil attack would allow us to surround a node and prevent its transactions from being flooded across the network. This would effectively render that node unable to participate. The solution to this is to vary the connections that each node makes so that it does not stay connected to the same set of nodes for an extended period.

A Sybil attack can also be used in privacy attacks by making many identities that belong to you. In this way, you can reduce the anonymity set of the transaction by eliminating your accounts from the list. Imagine, for

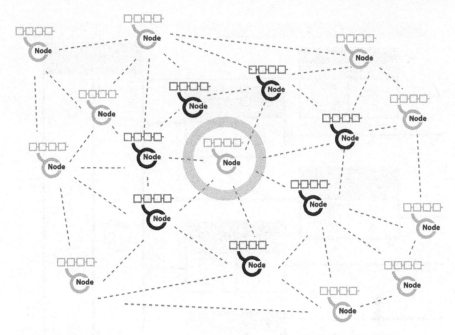

Figure 13.9 Sybil attack.

example, that I am mixing my coins using a technique as described in the previous section on privacy. I am adding say 10 coins to a mixed wallet and passing them to a second wallet that I do not wish to be linked.

Unbeknownst to me, however, someone has flooded the network with transactions to be mixed. They know where those coins are going from and going to. This means that when they look at the transactions on the blockchain, they can now eliminate their transactions from the anonymity set and link the two wallets together.

Figure 13.10 shows stripey accounts under my control. Because of this, I can determine that Account 3 sent funds to Account C.

CRYPTO-JACKING

This is the hijacking of someone's computer to mine cryptocurrency. Sometimes mining software is installed with some other application or it could be running in a browser when you are visiting a particular site. It uses your computer to generate hashes, stealing computing power to work for the attacker. It may seem innocuous enough, as it is not the most destructive form of malware when you compare it to other forms such as ransom-ware, but it increases the load on your computer, making your computer more costly to run and leaving it fewer resources to run other applications.

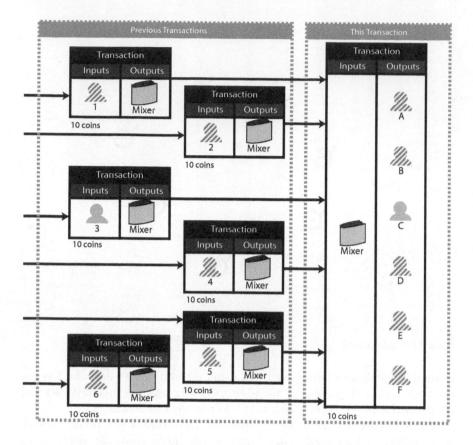

Figure 13.10 Sybil mixer attack.

IP ADDRESS MAPPING

Sometimes the aim of an attack is not to reverse transactions or affect the way that mining happens at all. Sometimes, the attacker may want to link accounts to real-world identities. This might be so that they can launch a real-world attack on high-value targets, for example, or follow up with phishing or other online attacks.

They can use a network of nodes and monitor the transaction traffic coming in from each node. Say I was very interested in identifying the owner of a particular account. I could monitor which transactions I receive from different nodes. I am looking to see which account seems to generate TXs, as when you create a TX it is propagated around the network. See the earlier section on Dandelions for more information on this and how to address it.

We can also use packet sniffing on unsecured internet connections. If I am watching the traffic on a network, I can monitor who receives and who transmits a particular transaction, associated with my account of interest. If you are the only node that broadcast the TX but did not receive the TX, then I can be sure that this account is yours.

DENIAL OF SERVICE, DoS ATTACK

A Denial of Service attack overloads the target with information to process. In the context of cryptocurrencies, this could be flooding the mempool with large numbers of zero-fee transactions or distributing large numbers of invalid blocks. They would be rejected, but the target system would have to download and inspect them before determining this, wasting time and resources.

There are several steps that cryptocurrencies can and do take to prevent this. They include distributing only valid blocks so that any invalid blocks can only make it so far as the first "honest node", limits on the number of free transactions and the temporary banning of misbehaving nodes.

Key points about blockchain attacks

- One of the most common attacks is to gain access to someone's private key.
- A 51 per cent attack is the name given to an attack that works through having more than half of the nodes being under the control of a single entity.
- This allows those nodes to perform malicious activities such as transaction reversal, selfish mining, transaction censoring and double-spending.
- Single-Shard-Takeover attack uses the same principles but does not require as many nodes.
- A Sybil attack is the name for an attack where multiple accounts are under the control of a single entity.
- Sybil attacks can be used to reduce or remove privacy, censoring of a given nodes transactions or double-spending.
- Crypto-Jacking is the use of malicious code to use other people's computers to mine for you without permission.
- A Denial of Service attack floods a network or node with more information than it can cope with, in order to stop it from functioning correctly.

Closing words

Congratulations! If you have made it to the end of this book, then you know a lot more about blockchains and how they work than the vast majority of people! The blockchain field is changing rapidly and new applications and technologies are ever emerging, but what we have covered in this book will give you a great foundation from which to begin your journey.

If you have enjoyed this book and want to say hello, then you can find me ...

on Twitter @KiraSummers4

on LinkedIn Kira Summers

Glossary

51 per cent attack A blockchain based attack where one can exert influence over the contents of the blockchain by virtue of controlling the majority of hash power or nodes on the network.

A

Accidental forks Where there are two or more versions of the blockchain caused by different nodes successfully adding a block at the same block height before the other can be distributed.

Account model, Account/balance model A model of managing assets where account values are adjusted based on transactions.

Addresses Public keys or public key derived numbers typically shown in Base-58 or QR codes, capable of having blockchain based assets assigned to them.

AML See Anti-money laundering.

Anti-money laundering (AML) Legislation intended to limit money laundering.

Anonymity sets The set of possibilities, when trying to identify a person or account.

ASIC Stands for Application Specific Integrated Circuit. It is a device built specifically for the purpose, in this case creating hash solution for Proof of Work.

Asymmetric encryption Encryption where two keys are used, one for encryption and one for decryption.

B

Base-16 A numeric system where there are 16 unique characters which represent numbers.

Base-58 A numeric system where there are 58 unique characters which represent numbers.

Base-64 A numeric system where there are 64 unique characters which represent numbers.

Binary A numeric system where there are two unique characters which represent numbers.

Bitcoin The original blockchain based cryptocurrency.

Blocks The segments into which transaction data is divided on a blockchain.

Block height The sequential position of a block on the blockchain.

Block reward The reward paid to the successful node when a block is added to the blockchain.

Block time The time in between blocks being added to the blockchain.

Blockchain 2.0 A term given to blockchains the accommodate the use of smart contracts

Brute force A type of attack based on trying many options in repetition until one is successful.

Burning The destruction of tokens on a blockchain network.

Bytecode Code compiled to run on a virtual machine.

C

CA See "Certificate Authority".

CDP See "Collateralized Debt Position".

Censoring transactions The ability to limit a person or accounts capacity to have transactions added to the blockchain by virtue of controlling a significant number of the hash power of the network.

Certificate Authority (CA) A body that issue certificates enabling a person or application access to a permissioned blockchain.

Certificate Revocation List (CRL) A list of all of the certificates that have been revoked and are no longer able to access a permissioned blockchain.

Certificates A digital document which contains information about the certificate holder and a public key, coupled to a private key held by the certificate holder, which they can use to verify their identity.

Chain code an equivalent to "smart contract" code that executes on a permissioned blockchain.

Chain of Trust The trust relationship between Certificate Authorities and certificates, where the revocation of a certificate will invalidate all certificates issued by the revoked entity and all Certificate Authorities certificated by it.

Channels A blockchain network that is part of a permissioned blockchain. Each node can be members of multiple channels.

CoinJoin A technique to increase privacy for blockchain transactions where transactions are merged together.

Cold wallets Wallets that are not connected to the internet.

Collateralized Debt Position (CDP) Where one can obtain an asset by locking in another as collateral, and receive the initial asset back, when the debt is returned.

Collisions Where one happens to select a value that is already in use.

Confidential transactions A method for increasing privacy in cryptocurrencies where the value of the transaction is obscured.

Confirmations The number of blocks added after your transaction. This is counted with the first block being the one in which your transaction is contained.

Consensus mechanisms The mechanism by which nodes come to agreement on the true contents of the blockchain.

CRL See Certificate Revocation List.

Cryptocurrencies Currencies that are built on blockchain networks.

Crypto-jacking The covert subversion of a victim's computer to mine cryptocurrencies for the attacker.

CryptoNote A privacy centric cryptocurrency.

D

Dai A stable coin that maintains its value through the use of dollar denominated collateralized debt positions.

Dandelion A technique where a transaction is passed around a number of nodes prior to flooding, in order to obscure its origin location.

DApps Shorthand for Decentralized Applications.

Dash coin A privacy coin which allows but does not enforce the use of some privacy measures.

Decentralized Applications, DApp Applications that are stored on the blockchain and are executed by virtual machines on the node.

Decentralized Autonomous Organization, DAO An organization which runs autonomously through the use of blockchain technologies.

Decentralized computing A computing system where resources and activities are distributed across the nodes on the network.

Delegated Proof of Stake A Proof of Stake based consensus mechanism which uses stakes to determine votes and control of the system.

DeFi An abbreviation of Decentralised Finance. This is where a financial service is provided in a decentralised manner, enabled through blockchain technology and smart contracts.

Denial of Service, DoS An attack which aims to disrupt the victim's connection to the internet.

Difficulty A value which controls how difficult it is to find a successful hash and add a block to the blockchain.

Difficulty Target The value that the block hash must fall under in order to be a valid block.

Distributed Ledger Technology, DLT   A Decentralized network with blockchain that contains a ledger.

Double-spend   Where one can spend the same currency more than once.

DPoS   See "Delegated Proof of Stake".

E

ECC   See "Elliptic Curve Digital Signature Algorithm".

ECDSA   See "Elliptic Curve Digital Signature Algorithm".

Elliptic Curve Cryptography   See "Elliptic Curve Digital Signature Algorithm".

Elliptic Curve Digital Signature Algorithm (ECDSA)   A system used for encryption and digital signatures based on elliptic curves. Also known as Elliptic Curve Cryptography (ECC).

Encryption   The encoding of data so it becomes secret to those who cannot decode it.

ERC1155   An Ethereum token type that supports fungible and non-fungible tokens.

ERC20   An Ethereum token type that supports fungible tokens.

ERC721   An Ethereum token type that supports non-fungible tokens.

Ethereum   A blockchain that was design to allow the use of smart contracts. Its native coin is ETH, but it is capable of supporting many other token types.

Ethereum Virtual Machine, EVM   The virtual machine that runs on Ethereum nodes that executes the bytecode.

EVM   See "Ethereum Virtual Machine".

F

Faucets   Services that dispense free tokens for testing.

Fiat currencies   Currencies that are not tied to a hard asset such as gold. They are not backed up by an asset with limited supply and it is therefore possible to "print money".

Flooding   The distribution of a transaction across the network into the mempools of the nodes.

Forks   Where nodes on the blockchain network do not have consensus on the one true version of the blockchain.

Full nodes   A node with a complete copy of the blockchain.

Fungible   An item type where one time is interchangeable for another.

G

Ganache   An application for testing smart contract where code is executed on a local test system.

Gas   The fee paid to execute commands on the Ethereum network.

H

Halvening   "See Halving".

Halving   An even which happens every four years approximately, where the block reward for Bitcoin is reduced by half.

Hard forks   A divergence of nodes on a blockchain network, which results in there being two distinct and stable versions of the blockchain.

Hardware wallets   A piece of hardware containing the private keys, where the key never leaves the devices. Instead it signs transactions inside the devices and provides these signed transactions for distribution across the blockchain.

Hash   See "Hashing".

Hash power   The capacity to produce hashes.

Hash rate   The rate at which hashes are produced.

Hashing   A mathematical function which for given data produces a number which is typically represented alphanumerically. A set input will always result in the same output.

HD wallets   See "Hierarchical Deterministic wallets".

Hierarchical Deterministic wallets allow for the generation of many different wallet addresses from the same keys.

Hexadecimal   See Base-16.

HODL   A slang term for "hold", sometimes said as Hold on for Dear Life. Commonly pronounces like the word Hoddle.

Hosted wallets   Wallets that are provided through a thirds party service where they custody your coins and keys.

Hot wallets   A wallet connected to the internet.

Hyperledger   A commonly used permissioned blockchain framework.

Immutability   The property of being unchangeable.

Intermediate Certificate Authority, ICA   A certificate authority created by another certificate authority.

I

IP address mapping   The activity of mapping IP addresses to known individuals or groups.

J

JavaScript   A commonly used programming language for the web.

K

Keccak-256   An encryption and signing method.

Know Your Customer (KYC)   Legislation and guidance requiring the knowledge of which accounts are associated with which people or groups.
KYC   See "Know Your Customer".

L

Layer Two solutions   A framework built on blockchain as Layer One.
Ledgers   A record of accounting, debt and credit.
Lightning Network   A Layer Two solution designed to address scaling of the Bitcoin network.
Locking scripts   A script that locks a transaction, restricting who can spent it or how it can be spent.

M

Magic number   An identifier of the blockchain network.
Maker DAO   Is an Ethereum-based Decentralized Autonomous Organization which provides lending and borrowing services.
MD5   A hashing function which has been found to have several vulnerabilities.
Membership Service Provider (MSP)   Provides approval for the actions of identities on a permissioned blockchain, based on their certificate.
Mempool   The pool of transactions each node holds that are waiting for inclusion in the blockchain.
Merkle root   The end result of an iterative process of hashing different values together.
Merkle tree   The tree of hashes produced when iteratively hashing different pieces of data and then hashing their hashes together until one ends up with a Merkle root.
Metadata   Data the describes other data.
Mining   The process of looking for hashes in order to add blocks to the blockchain.
Mining pools   The grouping together of hashing power into a pool, sharing the hash power and sharing the rewards.
Minting   The production of new tokens for a cryptocurrency.
Mixer   The process designed break the link between UTXOs and their origin whereby multiple coin are added together and output to multiple addresses.
Monero   A privacy-based cryptocurrency.
MSP   See "Membership Service Provider".

N

NFT   See "non-fungible tokens".
Nodes   A computer on the blockchain network.

Nonce A nonsense number, a number used only once, which can be varied in order to allow for different hash results.

Non-custodial wallets A wallet where you do not control the keys and do not directly control the tokens/coins.

Non-fungible tokens (NFT) A token which is not interchangeable for other tokens.

O

On-chain analysis The processes of reviewing data on the blockchain in order to extract further meaning.

Ordering service A service in permission blockchains where the contents of the blockchain are sequenced before being added, avoiding forks.

Overflow Where there are more digits than a given storage space in memory can accommodate. Can be used in attacks on vulnerable smart contracts.

P

Partial nodes A node which has an incomplete version of the blockchain.

PBFT See "Practical Byzantine Fault Tolerance".

Pederson commitments A mathematical technique using elliptic curve cryptography, used in confidential transactions.

Permissioned blockchains Blockchain networks which require authorization to access data and perform operations.

Permissionless blockchains Blockchains that do not require permission or certification to interact with. Anyone can generate addresses.

PoA See "Proof of Authority".

PoET See "Proof of Elapsed Time".

PoRe See "Proof of Reputation".

PoS See "Proof of Stake".

PoW See "Proof of Work".

Practical Byzantine Fault Tolerance Is a consensus mechanism named after the "Byzantine Generals' Problem".

Privacy coins Cryptocurrencies which attempt to protect the user's privacy around some aspect of sending, receiving or the amounts transacted.

Private blockchains Blockchains that are not open to the public.

Private keys Part of an encryption mechanism, which together with the public key allow for encryption and digital signatures.

PrivateSend A method of increasing privacy through merging transactions used in Dash coin.

Proof of Authority (PoA) A consensus mechanism where a node can contribute if it can establish authorization to do so.

Proof of Elapsed Time (PoET)   A consensus mechanism designed to reduce energy consumption which relies on randomized timers to select which nodes add blocks.

Proof of Reputation (PoRe)   A consensus mechanism where a node can contribute staking its reputation to do so.

Proof of Stake (PoS)   A consensus mechanism whereby nodes are selected to add blocks to the blockchain based on their staked funds.

Proof of Work (PoW)   A consensus mechanism whereby nodes are able to add blocks to the blockchain based on their finding of a valid nonce and hash.

Protocols   A set of rules that govern operation.

Provenance   Proof of history and/or ownership.

Public blockchains   Blockchain networks that do not require approval to interact with.

Public keys   Part of an encryption mechanism, which together with, together with the private key allow for encryption and digital signatures.

Public Key Infrastructure (PKI)   A set of tools and techniques for management of digital certificates.

Q

QR codes   An abbreviation of Quick Response codes. An encoding of text as a block-based graphic which is machine readable.

R

RCA   See "Root Certificate Authority".

Re-entrancy   An Attack based on re-entering code.

Remix, Remix IDE   An Integrated Development Environment (IDE) for the development of smart contracts.

Ring signatures   A privacy technique where several possible transactions are offered as the input and only one is valid.

RingCT   The collective term for Ring Signatures and Confidential Transactions.

Root Certificate Authority (RCA)   The first and founding Certificate Authority in a Chain of Trust.

S

Sat   See "Satoshi".

Satoshi   The name given to the smallest divisible amount of Bitcoin. Named after the creator of Bitcoin.

Satoshi Nakamoto   The assumed pseudonymous creator of Bitcoin.

ScriptPubKey A script that locks a transaction, restricting who can spent it or how it can be spent.

ScriptSig A signature that unlocks a transaction for spending.

Seed phrases A list of words used to generate a key set, to create a wallet.

Selfish mining A mining activity whereby blocks are not distributed to the network immediately, which allows the miner to mine all the blocks.

SHA-256 or Secure Hash Algorithm 256 is a hashing algorithm used by Bitcoin and other cryptocurrencies.

Shadow mining See "Selfish mining".

Sharding A technique for allowing blockchains to scale where nodes are split into smaller segments or "shards" each handling a portion of the network activity.

Shared keys An encryption technique where a key is shared between the two communicating parties.

Simplified payment verification (SPV) See "Partial node".

Single-Shard-Takeover attack An attack where a shard is controlled dishonestly.

Smart contracts The name given to the code that is stored on the blockchain and executed by its virtual machine.

Sock-puppets Multiple accounts under the control of the same entity, used in attacks.

Soft forks A fork which does not result in the creation of two distinct blockchains.

Solidity A language commonly used to create smart contracts.

SPV See "Partial node".

Stable coins Coins of stable value, typically associated with fiat currencies such as the dollar, the euro or the pound.

Stealth addresses A privacy technique for the obfuscation of the receiver's address.

Supply chain A chain of suppliers, transporters, vendors and other entities involved in the process of supply.

Sybil attack An attack based on the use of multiple accounts under an entity's control.

T

Testnet A network used for testing solutions.

Tokenization The association of a token with something, for example one can have a token represent houses, art, amounts of work, etc.

Transactions (TX) The reallocation of assets from one to another.

Tron A blockchain network and smart contract platform, Tron uses "energy" and "bandwidth" to pay for processing.

Truffle, Truffle Suite A commonly used suite of tools used in the development of DApps.

Tumblers   See "Mixers".
TX   See Transactions.

U

Unlocking scripts   A signature that unlocks a transaction for spending.
Unspent Transaction Output   This is the value of a transaction that has been sent, but not yet spent by the receiver.
Update forks   A fork caused when an update is rolled out to nodes on a blockchain network.
UTXO   See "Unspent Transaction Output".
UTXO model   A model of managing transactions based on the use of Unspent Transaction Outputs.

V

Virtual machines   Is an emulation of a computer.

W

Wallets   A suitable set of private and public keys that allow the holder to send and receive funds. Normally this is built into an application or service which assists the user in managing their funds.
World state   The name of the database summarizing the current state of the blockchain in permissioned blockchain systems.

X

X509 Standard   A standard used in the production of digital certificates.

Index